The Jeu de Paume Museum

Louvre Museum

The Jeu de Paume Museum

Translation
by **C. de Chabannes**

Catalogue drawn up
by **Hélène Adhémar**
Head Curator
and **Anne Dayez-Distel**
Curator

Fourth edition
revised and corrected

Ministère de la Culture et de la Communication.
Éditions de la Réunion des Musées Nationaux. Paris. 1980.

Cover:
Auguste RENOIR
Dancing in town
(detail). 1883.

Frontispiece:
Edouard MANET
Bullfight
(detail). 1865-66.

© Éditions de la Réunion des Musées Nationaux, Paris 1980.
© S.P.A.D.E.M. - A.D.A.G.P., Paris 1980.
ISBN 2.7118.0136.5.

● Colour reproduction
□ Enlarged detail

Preface

Towards the years 1862-1863, a group of young painters decided to rediscover nature. Instead of continuing to transpose it in the light of their studios, they would set up their easels in the open air. Making use of new discoveries in the field of science, they juxtaposed pure colours and thus obtained values which enabled them to render *sensation, atmosphere, impression*. Corot and Delacroix had shown the way (Fantin-Latour expressed their gratitude to Delacroix just after the Master's death in his **Tribute to Delacroix**). Manet was to be at the centre of this group of young artists, which Fantin commemorated a few years later in **The Studio at Les Batignolles.** He exhibited **Lunch on the Grass** and **Bathing** at the ''Salon of the Rejected'' in 1963, but the Emperor preferred Cabanel's **Birth of Venus,** which he bought at the official Salon. A comparison of the two works shows how disconcerting was this new art which rejected all pictural artifices and relied on contrast and the opposition of colours applied with wide brush-strokes. Two years later, at the Salon of 1865, the critics attacked **Olympia** even more violently. Amidst all this incomprehension, however, a few voices were raised in defense of Manet, while Zola wrote with surprising foresight that ''Fate has without doubt already chosen the Louvre as the future home of **Olympia** and **Lunch on the Grass.**

Bazille, Monet, Sisley and Renoir were more attracted to the open air than was Manet. They would meet in the Forest of Fontainebleau, where Daubigny had been one of the first to set up his easel. They received advice from Courbet and Diaz, whom they also met in Normandy, where Boudin and Jongkind helped them to discover the sea.

These years of intense work, during which they were often living in great poverty, gave birth to works which attracted as yet little notice from the public. The 1870 Salon, the last of the Second Empire, saw the triumph of Regnault's **Salomé.** Cézanne had submitted the portrait of his friend **Emperaire** (admittedly in a spirit of bravado) to the same Salon, where it was naturally refused.

War broke out shortly after and the group was dispersed. Bazille, killed at Beaune-la-Rolande, was not to return. When the others came back from exile in Holland or

England, their talent had matured. It was with renewed joy of living that they would meet at Argenteuil or in the Ile-de-France to compare enthusiastically the result of their researches. The works of this period are undoubtedly amongst the most luminous of their careers.

In 1874, the group decided to show their work in public. For this, they rented the studio of the photographer Nadar (35, boulevard des Capucines) from 15th April to 15th May. This exhibition succeeded in arousing the curiosity of the public and revealed the extent of incomprehension amongst the critics. It was one of them who, faced with Monet's **Impression, rising sun,** applied to them the term **Impressionists.** The expression, which had first been used in mockery, was soon adopted by the artists themselves, for whom it became a password and who gloried in it. Monet, Pissarro, Renoir, Sisley, Guillaumin, were all in love with nature and strove tirelessly to represent its most fleeting aspects, leaving marvellous paintings which bear witness to their virtuosity. Degas, Manet, Cézanne were more attracted by the psychological aspect of their subjects and their universe is one which tends to arouse reflection. The year 1882 saw the appearance of new tendencies. Seurat's experiments, his theory of *divisionism,* gained him an adept in Pissarro, the veteran of the Impressionists, who had taught Cézanne to use a light palette and encouraged Gauguin.

In 1886, the group broke up, after the eighth and last Impressionist exhibition.

Gauguin attracted followers in Pont-Aven, which he abandoned temporarily for the Martinique, then permanently for Tahiti. Van Gogh arrived from the North with his visions of destitution, to be dazzled by the beauty of the landscapes of the Ile-de-France. Like Toulouse-Lautrec, with his witty, caustic talent, he was to take part in the life of the art students and cafés of the period before he left for the South, where there was "more colour, more sun."

All these painters felt an absolute need for light and their colours became increasingly intense. Mallarmé was amazed that Gauguin's work could contain "such great mystery

within such great brilliance." Van Gogh, Cézanne, used colour to ennoble form. Vincent was to attain a degree of lyricism which destroyed him. Cézanne proceeded with greater prudence, passing from Impressionism, in which he lingered only for a short time, through a constructive and powerfully monumental period, and finally confused intermingled forms and colours, achieving an extraordinarily luminous density in which lyricism is controlled by a rigourously constructed rhythm.

Degas, Monet and Renoir did not express themselves in the same way, but their researches were identical. Degas paints the fluctuation of light on the movements of a dancer, and Renoir on the body of a **girl bathing,** just as Monet does in his "series" of landscapes or **cathedrals** seen at different times of day. As they grew older, their colours became increasingly vivid, as if they were making a tragic effort to transcribe light at its maximum intensity before their eyesight became less acute. Degas, Renoir and Monet lived long enough to see the creation of various movements born in reaction to their own theories, which were nevertheless at the root of these new tendencies.

A few enlightened connaisseurs had discerned the genius of these young painters from the first and constituted collections which they generously donated to the State. It is thanks to them that it has been possible to assemble such a distinguished ensemble. Sometimes there were friends like Caillebotte or Bazille—painters themselves but financially better off—who bought their works or gave material help, saving them from despair and enabling them to continue their work. The names of these generous benefactors are inscribed on one wall of the Jeu de Paume, and certain rooms are named after great collectors like Moreau-Nélaton, Camondo, Pellerin, Personnaz, Gachet, Mollard, Kaganovitch, who are thus gratefully remembered together with the artists.

The building originally contained an Orangery, like the one symetrical to it in the direction of the Seine. Its present name comes from the "jeu de paume" or tennis-court, installed by Napoleon III on the terrace of "Les Feuillants" for his son, the Imperial Prince. It was fitted up by the architect Viraut and inaugurated on 29 January 1862. The tennis court was enlarged several times and was used for exhibitions at the beginning of the twentieth century, when the "jeu de paume" was replaced by modern tennis. The first was held in 1909, showing "One hundred portraits of women from the English and French Schools of the nineteenth century." Exhibitions succeeded each other, year after year. Among the most important was the Dutch Exhibition of 1921, in which figured eight Van Goghs and Vermeer's **View of Delft,** which Proust came to view, as did his own Bergotte, paying for the visit with an attack of asthma.

By 1924, Léonce Bénédite, Curator of the Luxembourg Museum (who had thought of placing Monet's **Water-lilies** there and creating an Impressionist centre in the Orangerie) began planning the removal of his museum's foreign collections to the Jeu de Paume. It was not till 1932 that the foreign paintings were installed in the renovated rooms, and part of the building was left free for the temporary exhibitions which were held there until 1941. During the War, the foreign collections were housed in the Museum of Modern Art and the Museum in Compiègne. The Nazis stored the collections they seized in France in the Jeu de Paume, before transporting them to Germany and they were returned there in 1945 before being restored to their owners by the Department for the Recuperation of National Art Treasures.

It was after the war, in 1947, that M. René Huyghe, who was then Curator of the Department of Paintings, had the Impressionist collections moved from the Louvre to the Jeu de Paume "bathed through its numerous windows and bays, in the living light which was the discovery and the obsession of these painters. This is not the too-regular, rather solemn lighting of a museum, but a light still tremulous from its contact with the leaves, lawns and pools on which the Jeu de Paume opens on every side." In 1954, M. Germain

Bazin made extensive alterations to the museum so as to permit the installations essential to its function: climatisation, lighting, better presentation of the paintings, the number of which had greatly increased.

In 1969, the rooms were renovated once more. The works were arranged in chronological order, but not rigourously so, since it was necessary to preserve the harmony of the presentation and occasionally to take into account conditions imposed by the donor. We were able, however, to use a subterfuge. Where a collection must obligatorily remain grouped together, an opening has been made in the room so as to link it with works by the same painters on show in the museum. This has been done in the case of the Manets of the Moreau-Nélaton collection, the Degas' of the Camondo collection and the Cézanne's of the Gachet collection. Furthermore, the Antonin Personnaz collection, which had remained in the Louvre, has been moved to the Jeu de Paume, where a room has recently been allocated to the Dr. Eduardo Mollard Donation, and another to the Max and Rosy Kaganovitch Donation.

The Department of Art Objects and the Museum of African and Oceanic Arts have loaned sculptures by Gauguin and these, together with panels and stained glass, have enabled us to present, in the room where his paintings are collected, an unique ensemble of the Master's art, showing all his forms of expression.

The reorganisation and regrouping has made it possible to emphasise the exceptional importance of the work of the great Impressionist painters.

We are very much looking forward to having a larger building in which to house them. We shall then be able to give more space to each work and besides the exhibition rooms, we shall have the audio-visual rooms indispensable for recounting the history of the movement and making known the works of these artists. We also hope for rooms in which to hold lectures and discussions, so that the works shown in the museum itself may be contemplated in silence.

Hélène Adhémar

Bazille

Jean-Frédéric
1841-1870

The pink dress, also know as View of Castelnau. 1864.

The Forest of Fontainebleau. 1865.

The makeshift ambulance. 1865.

Family reunion. 1867.

Portrait of Renoir. 1867.

☐ The artist's studio. 1870.

Bazille arrived in Paris in 1862 and worked in Gleyre's studio, where he met Claude Monet. He became friendly with Cézanne, Guillaumin, Sisley, Zola, Solari and above all Monet and Renoir. He was influenced by Courbet, whom he greatly admired, but even more so by Manet. He was also interested in the researches of Boudin, Corot, Th. Rousseau. In 1865, he was one of the models for Monet's **Lunch on the Grass** and attended the meetings at the café Guerbois. He exhibited at the Salons of 1866, 1868, 1869 and 1870.

He enlisted during the war of 1870 and was killed in the same year during the battle of Beaune-la-Rolande (Loiret).

Studies in light and the open air and experiments in the use of a light palette ensure him a place among the pioneers of Impressionism. Bazille also became one of the first patrons of Impressionist painting when, in 1867, he bought Monet's **Women in the Garden** (R.F. 2773). His comrades owed much to his generous and disinterested help, which enabled them to overcome their financial difficulties during these early days of Impressionism.

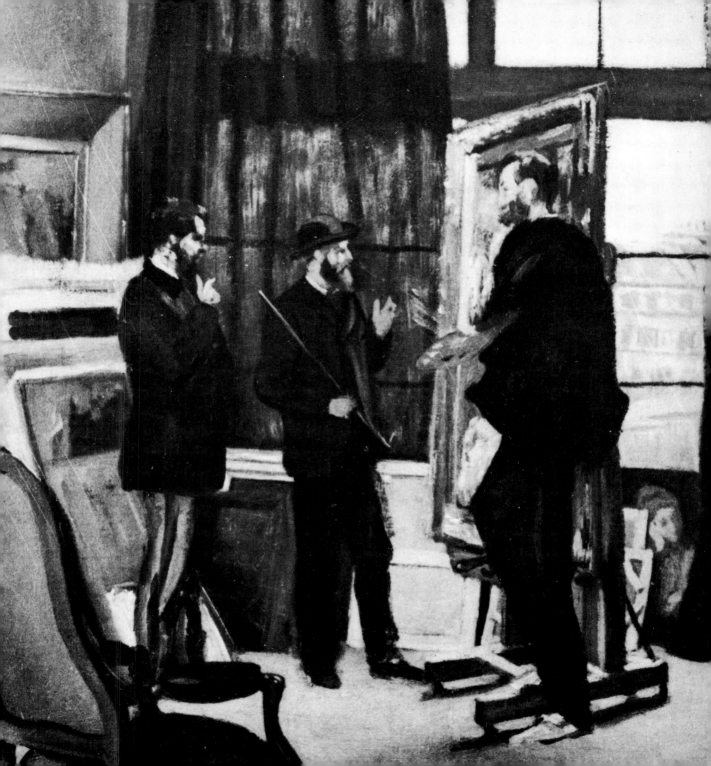

Boudin

Louis-Eugène
1824-1898

● The beach at Trouville. 1864.

The beach at Trouville. 1865.

The beach at Trouville. 1867.

Bathers on the beach at Trouville. 1869.

The harbour at Antwerp. 1871.

Boudin had been councelled by Isabey and Troyon and greatly impressed by the art of Corot and Courbet, but it was Jongkind who influenced him most strongly. He was an open-air painter, an attentive observer of the sky and the sea, executing numerous studies in pastel or oils of the changing aspects of the atmosphere.

He was Monet's first master in Le Havre. In about 1860, when he was living in Honfleur, he frequented the group of the «Ferme Saint-Siméon» — the rustic inn to which he brought Courbet, and where Diaz, Troyon, Cals, Daubigny and Corod had stayed. In 1874, he took part in the first Impressionist exhibition. Boudin also worked in Britanny, in the South of France, in Bordeaux, Belgium, Holland and Venice.

From 1861, he spent the winter in Paris, but worked from nature in summer, travelling widely.

The Impressionist Exhibition of 1874 was the only one in which Boudin took part. Thereafter, he preferred to show his work at the Salon. Nevertheless, his dealer, Paul Durand-Ruel, was also that of the Impressionists. He held several one-man shows for Boudin (1833, 1889, 1890, 1891).

Boudin

The beach at Trouville.

Boudin was born in Honfleur and died in Deauville. His name is inseparably linked with his canvases portraying the Normandy beaches.

A scholarship accorded by the municipality of Le Havre enabled him to study for three years in Paris (1851-1854). He had a profound admiration for Corot and wished to devote himself to landscape. Returning to Le Havre, Boudin set out to depict the coast and ports of Normandy, painting from life. The only variety in the painter's motifs are introduced by his stays in Paris and journeys to Britanny, Bordeaux and the South of France, and even to Venice, Holland, etc. From 1856 on, his diary shows what he was seeking for: "Swim in the open sky. Reach the "tenderness" of the clouds. Suspend these masses in the background, far distant in the grey mist, bring out the sparkle of blue..."

Towards 1862, he began work on a special theme: that of the beaches animated by the throng of elegant holiday-makers who were beginning to frequent Deauville and Trouville in summer—paintings which are almost subject-pictures. He accumulated water-color studies, done from life, mere sketches for finished works like this **Beach at Trouville,** dating from 1864, in which Boudin recaptures the gay, worldly atmosphere of the fashionable beaches. The rather superficial subject leaves him free to express himself according to his own sensibility. This light-toned painting, which reveals every detail of the vibration of light, had a profound influence on the young Claude Monet, who was also a native of Le Havre. "It is due to Eugène Boudin that I became a painter" he declared, thus revealing the important part played by Boudin in the birth of Impressionism.

This small panel is certainly one of the most charming works in the collection formed by Eduardo Mollard. The greater part of this collection has been grouped in the Jeu de Paume thanks to a donation made in 1861, followed by a bequest in 1972. This connaisseur's perceptive choice of painters of the latter half of the nineteenth century, shows how they treated the theme of light.

The beach at Trouville. 1864.

Boudin

The harbour at Camaret. 1872.

Landscape with washerwomen. 1873.

The harbour at Bordeaux. 1874.

The harbour at Bordeaux. 1874.

Seascape. 1881.

Sailings-boats. 1885-90.

The harbour at Le Havre. 1888.

The jetty at Deauville. 1889.

●□ Venice. La riva dei Schiavoni. 1895.

Caillebotte

Gustave
1848-1894

The floor-planers. 1875.

Rooftops in the snow. 1878.

Henri Cordier. 1883.

Sailing-boats at Argenteuil. 1888.

Self-portrait. 1889.

Caillebotte came from a well-off family of the Parisian bourgeoisie. He worked in Bonnard's studio and was admitted to the School of Fine Arts in 1873. At about the same time, he came into contact with the Impressionnists and abandonned official teaching to join their group. In 1876, he took part in the second Impressionist exhibition and became from that time on, one of the animators of the movement as well as a veritable patron for his comrades.

His early paintings are realistic scenes from contemporary life and views of Paris. Towards 1882, under the influence of Monet, he devoted himself to landscape painting and executed numerous views of the Seine at Argenteuil.

He left his large collection, exclusively composed of Impressionnist painters, to the Louvre, thus opening to them the doors of the National Museums.

Cassatt

Mary
1844-1926

Woman sewing. 1886.

The daughter of a rich Pittsburg banker, she came in 1868 to work in Paris, where she became a pupil of Chaplin. She visited Italy, Spain and Belgium. Degas guided and councelled her. In 1879, she took part in the group's fourth exhibition and encouraged Mme Havemeyer to take an interest in the work of her friends. Her colouring is Impressionist, but she also sought the delicacy of line she found in Japanese prints and the work of Degas. She was almost blind when she died in 1926 at the Chateau de Beaufresne at Mesnil-Théribus (Oise).

Cézanne

Paul
1839-1906

Head of an old man. 1866.

Mary Magdalen also known as Suffering. 1868-69.

Still-life with kettle. 1869.

Achille Emperaire. 1868.

The strangled woman. 1870-72.

Cézanne began to work in Paris in 1862 at the Académie Suisse, where he met Pissarro and Guillaumin. At the café Guerbois, he became friendly with the group, which was dominated by the personality of Manet. There he also renewed acquaintance with E. Zola, his childhood friend. From 1863 to 1870, he divided his time between Paris and Aix. This first period, known as ''romantic'' or ''baroque'', reflects his admiration for Delacroix and Venetian Mannerism. From 1872 to 1874, he lived at Auvers-sur-Oise and was initiated under the influence of Pissarro into the use of a light palette. He took part in the Impressionist exhibitions of 1874 and 1877 From 1882 he lived alone at Aix-en-Provence where he formulated his ideas, going beyond Impressionnism and elaborating a solidly constructed art in which colour translates the plenitude of form. This style of treatment became increasingly lyrical towards the end of his life. In 1895, Vollard gave a great exhibition of his work. This was ill received by the general public but was hailed as a revelation by the young artists who considered him as their master. After 1904, he exhibited at the Salon d'Automne, where a retrospective exhibition of his work was held in 1907.

Cézanne

The village road at Auvers. 1872-73.

Doctor Gachet's house at Auvers. 1873.

The house of the hanged man. 1873.

The crossing at the Rue Rémy in Auvers. 1873.

●□ A modern Olympia. 1873.

The artist's accessories. Still-life with medallion of Philippe Solari. 1873.

Bouquet with a yellow dahlia. 1873.

Green apples. 1873.

Cézanne

Apples and Oranges.

This still-life, bequeathed by Isaac de Camondo, who died in 1911, was one of the first of Cézanne's works to enter the French collections open to the public. A few years after his death (1906) Cézanne made his entry into the Louvre. Yet the artist had been little appreciated by the public during his lifetime and had found favour only with a small group of connaisseurs, which had been slightly enlarged by Vollard's retrospective exhibition in 1895.

The still-life was always a favourite theme of Cézanne's. This one, which belongs to the artist's last period (ap. 1895-1900) sums up the artistic theories conceived during the course of his life. All Cézanne's still-lives describe ordinary objects, that are part of everyday life. Their very simplicity brings out by contrast the plastic quality of the forms and the play of light on the objects, which is the real theme of the picture. Cézanne abandons the traditional laws of perspective and constructs an ideal space which each object helps to determine. I, May 1904, he wrote in a letter to Emile Bernard: "The writer expresses himself by means of abstractions, whereas the painter concretises his sensations and perceptions in line and colour. One is not over-scrupulous, nor over-sincere, nor over-submissive to nature, but one has more or less mastered one's model, and above all one's means of expression. One must enter into the object one is observing and strive to express it in the most logical manner possible."

Cézanne always denied that he was an abstract theorician and insisted on the absolute necessity for a painter to force himself to "make a concrete study of nature": "The true, prodigious study we have to undertake, is that of the diversity we see in the canvas of nature," he wrote (letter to Emile Bernard, 12 May 1904). Nevertheless, his art has been the starting point for all the artistic theories of the 20th century.

Apples and Oranges.

Cézanne

Flowers in a Delft vase. 1873.

Dahlias. 1873.

□ Self-portrait. 1873–76.

Self-portrait. 1877–80.

Still-life with soup-tureen. 1877.

L'Estaque. 1878–79.

The bridge at Maincy. 1879–80.

Farmyard at Auvers. 1879–80.

Poplars. 1879–80.

The blue vase. 1885-87.

Still-life with basket. 1888-90.

The card-players. 1890-95.

Fishing-boat (fragment) *ap.* 1890.

Bathers. 1890-92.

Bathers. 1890-1900.

Woman with a coffee-pot.
1890-95.

Still-life with onions. 1895.

● Apples and Oranges. 1895-1900.

Degas

Hilaire-Germain-Edgar
1834-1917

Self-portrait. 1854-55.

Hilaire-René de Gas. 1857.

Marguerite de Gas. 1858-60.

Marguerite de Gas. 1858-60.

Giovanna Bellelli. 1856.

Study of hands.

☐ The Bellelli Family. 1858-60.

He came of a family of bankers which had settled in Naples since 1789. In 1854, he was trained for the School of Fine Arts by Lamothe, a pupil of Ingres and Flandrin. He entered it the following year, but remained for a short time only.

From 1856 to 1857, he was in Rome and Naples, where he studied the Primitives. Under the influence of Ingres, he painted historical subjects and portraits and until 1870 he contributed regularly to the Salon with works which were apparently in the traditional spirit. However, an acute feeling for "modernism," a taste for original layout, a desire to render the instantaneity of movement, followed by the discovery of pastel and colour, led him to join the group of painters and writers in the café Guerbois.

From 1874 on, he exhibited regularly with the Impressionists (except in 1882), but in 1886, his obstinate individualism separated him for ever from the group. He travelled widely in Europe (Italy, England, Belgium, Holland and Spain) as well in America (1872-73 he made a long stay in New Orleans, where part of his family had settled).

After 1890, Degas' sight began to fail and he gradually abandoned painting for pastel, monotype and sculpture. He died in Paris in 1917.

Degas

Semiramis founding Babylone. 1861.

Semiramis founding Babylone. 1861.

Gentleman's-Rider's race.
Before the start. 1862.

Thérèse de Gas. 1863.

Degas and Valernes. 1864.

Battle-scene during the Middle Ages. 1865.

Portrait of a young woman.
1867.

Evariste de Valernes. 1868.

The cellist Pillet. 1868-69.

Degas

The Star, or Dancer on stage.

In 1868, Degas began interpreting the world of opera and musicians with **Musicians in the Orchestra**; in 1872, he depicted **The green-room at the Opera of the rue Le Peletier** and from that time on, he continually chose the subject of dancers on the stage, either haloed in the fairylike atmosphere of the show, or in an intimate attitude in the wings.

It was inevitable that Degas should be attracted to this realistic, contemporary subject. He was constantly preoccupied by the problem of how to express ephemeral movement at the instant it occurred; the contrasting and mysterious lighting effects peculiar to the theatre with its brilliant flashes of colour, corresponded moreover to his own form of sensibility. The small pastel entitled **The Star, or Dancer on the Stage** dates from 1878 and summarises admirably the artist's intentions. The skilfully asymetrical composition shows off to full advantage the airy silhouette of the dancer, caught in a beam of light; certain highly finished zones contrast, with faultless technique, with others which have been rapidly coloured in subtle tones that are intentionally dull or dazzling.

It is highly probable that when Degas was executing this pastel, he made use of a rough outline left on a sheet of paper by a monotone plate. This is a method used by engravers, but Degas frequently employed it and perfected it.

The Star,
or Dancer
on stage.

Degas

The orchestra of the Paris Opera. 1868-70.

Pagans with Auguste de Gas. 1869.

The Ironing-woman. 1869.

Cliffs by the Sea. 1869.

Study of sky.

Trees bordering a plain.

Mademoiselle Dihau at the piano. 1869-72.

Jeantaud, Linet, Lainé. 1871.

Woman with a vase. 1872.

The green-room at the Opera
of the rue Le Peletier. 1872.

The chiropodist. 1873.

Stage-rehearsal of ballet. 1874.

The dancing class. 1874.

Mme Jeantaud at her mirror. 1875.

At the café, also known
as Absinthe. 1874.

Dancer with bouquet, curtseying. 1877.

End of an arabesque. 1877.

● The star, also known as
Dancer on the stage. 1878.

Degas

At the Stock-Exchange. 1878-79.

●□ Racehorses in front of the stands. 1879.

The race-course.
Riders beside a carriage. 1880.

A singer. 1880.

Tall dancer, clothed.
1880.

Three studies for the head of a dancer.
ap. 1880.

Dancers going upstairs. 1886-90.

Woman in her bath
sponging her leg. 1883.

Ironing-women. 1884.

The tub. 1886.

After the bath.
Woman drying her feet. 1886.

Harlequin and Colombine.
1886-90.

Dancers in blue. 1890.

Woman washing in her tub. 1892.

Fantin-Latour

Henri
1836-1904

Woman reading. 1861.

Narcissi and tulips. 1862.

Homage to Delacroix. 1864.

● Flowers and fruit. 1865.

Antoine Vollon. 1865.

A pupil of his father, Jean-Théodore Fantin-Latour, and of Lecoq de Boisbaudran. He made numerous copies of the master-pieces in the Louvre. He was a friend and supporter of Manet and frequented the Café Guerbois, though he remained faithful to a moderate form of classicism. He was a portrait-painter, and depicter of familiar scenes, and is chiefly famous for his large group compositions. He was attracted by Whistler and made three stays in England (1859, 1861, 1864). There, he achieved great success as a painter of flowers and this became his chief subject towards the end of his life. Fantin-Latour was an enlightened amateur of music and part of his work, as well as numerous lithographs, were inspired by dreams or by music.

Fantin-Latour

Flowers and Fruit.

Fantin-Latour occupies a place apart in his period. He was a friend and supporter of Manet and the author of two canvases which constitute "manifestoes" of the avant-garde of the years 1860-1870: **Tribute to Delacroix** (1864) and above all **The Studio at Les Batignolles** (1870), where we see Renoir, Zacharie Astruc, Emile Zola, Edmond Maître, Bazille, Monet, etc., grouped round Manet standing before his easel. Fantin-Latour's style remained nevertheless moderately classical and never became Impressionist, in spite of the painter's friendship with his comrades. Fantin-Latour preferred interiors to landscape, choosing objects or figures painted in sombre tones with coppery lights, to which the red of a bunch of flowers or the white of a table-cloth lends occasional brilliance. Apart from portraits and, at a later period, allegories inspired by contemporary music and tinged with symbolism, Fantin-Latour painted numerous still-lives, composed of flowers, fruit and a few simple objects. These carefully elaborated compositions are extremely traditional and their charm resides essentially in their delicate colouring. Apart from certain works where the texture is heavier, they show a transparency evoking the enamel technique of ancient paintings. Fantin's still-lives are poetic and a little old-fashioned, and are thus surprising in the period of Renoir and Monet.

Flowers and fruit.

Fantin-Latour

Manet's studio in the Batignolles quarter.
1870.

□ Manet's studio in the Batignolles quarter.
1870.

A corner of the table. 1872.

Study of a female nude.
1872.

Victoria Dubourg. 1873.

The Dubourg Family. 1878.

Charlotte Dubourg. 1882.

Roses in a glass bowl. 1882.

Around the piano. 1885.

Adolphe Jullien. 1887.

Bedtime.

Night. 1897.

Gauguin

Paul
1848–1903

The Seine at Iéna Bridge. 1875.

Still-life with mandolin. 1885.

Washerwomen at Pont-Aven. 1886.

Harvest in Britanny. 1888.

Les Alyscamps. 1888.

"La Belle Angèle". 1889.

Gauguin was of Spanish-Peruvian descent through his mother and spent his childhood in Peru. He was obsessed by a longing for travel and believed at first that his vocation was to be a sailor. In 1871, however, he became a stock-broker and married in 1873. It was then that he began to paint for his own amusement. Pissarro introduced him to the Impressionists. In 1883, he abandoned his social life and his family to devote himself entirely to painting.

He left for Pont-Aven in 1887, then for the island of Martinique, where he encountered the ardent colours of Tropical nature. These two journeys caused Gauguin to turn away from Impressionism. The break came in 1888 during his second stay in Pont-Aven with E. Bernard and Sérusier, and his journey to Arles, when he stayed with Van Gogh. Gauguin was the originator of "Cloisonnisme" (the search for pure colour) and **Synthetism.** He frequented Symbolist circles. In 1891, he left for Tahiti, returning in 1893. In 1895, however, he departed for ever, to share the simple life of the natives of Tahiti. In 1901, he settled in Dominica, where he died in 1903.

Gauguin

The Schuffenecker Family. 1889.

Yellow haystacks. 1889.

Still-life with fan. 1889.

Women from Tahiti. 1891.

●□ The meal. 1891.

●Arearea. 1892.

Self-portrait. 1893.
(see page 7).

Portrait of W. Molard. 1893-94.

Breton landscape. (Le moulin David).
1894.

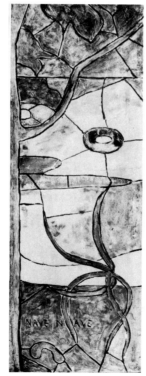

Floral and plant decorations. 1893.   Landscape with a tahitian girl. 1893.

Gauguin

Lintel of the carved door from Hiva-Oa hut.

Horizontal panel from Hiva-Oa hut.

Show-case. Carved woods and ceramics.

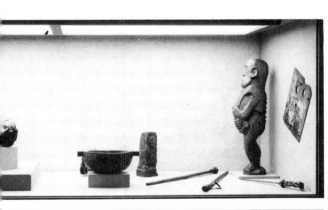

Vertical panel from Hiva-Oa Hut.

Gauguin

Arearea.

When Gauguin left for Tahiti en 1891, he had already formulated his artistic creed. He had named it "Synthetism" and had worked it out in Britanny, when he was staying at Pont-Aven, together with Emile Bernard. Gauguin had broken then with his Impressionist antecedents and begun to paint according to new principles, simplifiying his forms and employing large appliques of pure colour, clearly outlined. This intentionally decorative style was inspired by popular art (and also by the Japonese prints discovered by the Impressionists). These ideas corresponded, moreover, with the poetic definitions of the Symbolists, as did the themes and subjects illustrated by the painter. Gauguin, who had childhood memories of Peru and of his first journey to Martinique en 1887, abandoned the western world, seeking the impact of exotic scenes and primitive life. **Arearea** (Pleasantries) painted during the artist's first stay in Tahiti (1892) evokes a Tahitian ceremony. The artist has used one of his favourite proceedings: the figures and the dog in the foreground are not sharply disassociated from the procession passing like a frieze in a magical distance (the monumental idol was imagined by the artist, since he could have seen only small statuettes in Tahiti). This absence of relief, the simplicity of line and volume, the "barbarous" intensity of the colours, contribute to create a mysterious work, suggestive of things unknown or ill-explained.

This painting was exhibited by Durand-Ruel in 1898, when it aroused astonishment and admiration as well as mockery. Gauguin explained it later in the following terms: "I take as my pretext some subject from life or nature, then, by an arrangement of line and colour, I obtain symphonies and harmonies which represent absolutely nothing *real,* in the ordinary sense of the word. They do not directly express any idea. They should make people think in the same way as does music, without the help of ideas or images, simply by means of the mysterious affinities which exist between our brain and such arrangements of line and colour."

Arearea.

Gauguin

Breton village in the snow. 1894.

Peasant women from Brittany. 1894.

Self-portrait. 1896.

Vairumati. 1897.

The white horse. 1898.

"Et l'or de leur corps". 1901.

Gonzalès

Éva
1849–1883

A box at the Italiens theatre. 1874.

Eva Gonzalès was a pupil of Chaplin and above all of Manet, but she did not find it easy to follow the evolution towards painting in light tones. The colouring of her pastels is nevertheless very gentle and full of charm. She married the engraver Henri Guérard in 1878 and died prematurely.

Guillaumin

Armand
1841–1927

Lane under snow. 1869.

Canal boats on the Seine at Bercy. 1871.

Still-life. 1872.

Sunset over Ivry. 1873.

Paris, quai de Bercy. Snow effect. 1873.

Place Valhubert. Paris. 1875.

Born in Paris in 1841, of a family from Moulins. In 1864, he worked at the Académie Suisse, where he met Cézanne and Pissarro. He was an amateur painter and when he was employed in 1868 by the Department of Civil Engineering, he painted views of Paris and its suburbs.

In 1870, he began to make frequent visits to Dr. Gachet in Auvers-sur-Oise, who appreciated his work and remained a faithful friend. He continued to paint in the region of Paris (Damiette, Epinay-sur-Orge) the, from 1891 on, in the Creuse (Crozant) and the South (Agay). He made a journey to Holland in 1904.

Self portrait. 1875.

Nude woman, reclining. 1877.

Plain landscape. 1878.

The harbour at Charenton. 1878.

Fishermen. 1885.

Bend of a road after rain. 1887.

Landscape in Normandy: apple-trees. 1887.

View of Agay. 1895.

View of Holland. Sailing-boats. 1904.

Jongkind

Johan-Barthold
1819-1891

Ruins of the castle of Rosemont. 1861.

The Seine and Notre-Dame. 1864.

In Holland. Boats beside the windmill. 1868.

The Meuse at Dordrecht. 1870.

Rue de l'Abbé-de-l'Epée. 1872.

Jongkind never belonged to the Impressionist group or exhibited with it, but his influence on the painting of his period was nevertheless decisive. He came to France in 1846, staying several times in Honfleur and Le Havre (between 1847 and 1865). He was friendly with Boudin and Monet, who sought his advice. He also worked a great deal in Paris and in the Isère. In Jongkind we see the affirmation of the total change inaugurated by Corot and the Barbizon School in the conception of landscape painting, and a predeliction for expressing a fleeting atmosphere.

Lebourg

Albert-Charles
1849-1928

The harbour at Algiers. 1876.

Road beside the Seine, at Neuilly. 1888.

The lock of La Monnaie. Paris.

By the river Ain. 1897.

Snow at Pont-du-Château.

Steam-tugs at Rouen. 1903.

Lebourg was trained in an architect's studio and taught drawing at the Society for Fine Arts in Algiers from 1872 to 1876. He soon revealed himself as a talented landscape painter. He stayed for a time in Auvergne (1884-1888), but his preference was for the landscape of Normandy and he finally settled in Rouen, after travelling in Holland, Belgium, England and Switzerland. He frequented the Impressionists and exhibited with them in 1879 and 1880.

Lépine

Stanislas-Victor-Édouard
1836-1892

The port at Caen. 1859.

The artist's son.

Lighter alongside the quay.

The Seine at Charenton.

The embankments of the Seine,
Pont-Marie. 1868.

Landscape. 1869.

Montmartre, rue Saint-Vincent.

The apple-market. 1889.

Lépine was a pupil of Corot. He was imbued with the spirit of his master and had, like him, a profound love of nature. He made paintings of his birthplace, Caen, and also became known for his paintings of Paris, its quays and picturesque spots in the Butte Montmartre. He exhibited for the first time in 1859 and constantly presented his works at the Salons. Nevertheless, he remained little known to his contemporaries and took small part in the life of the group, though he exhibited with the Impressionnists in 1874. He was influenced by Jongkind, and like him, was a protégé of Count Doria, an influencial patron of the period.

Manet

Édouard
1832-1883

●□ Portrait of the artist's parents. 1860.

Lola de Valence. 1862.

□ Lunch on the grass. 1863.

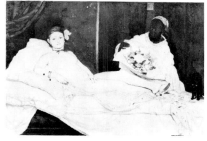

● Olympia. 1863.

Still-life: fruit on a table. 1864.

Stem of white peonies and secateurs. 1864.

Manet was the son of a magistrate and came of an upper middle-class family. He became a pupil in Couture's studio in 1849, but could not accept its conventional teaching, preferring to teach himself by copying master-pieces in museums in France and abroad (travels in Italy from 1853; in Germany and Holland, 1856). He was attracted by the Spanish art of the seventeenth century (Velasquez, Zurbaran, Murillo) and journeyed to Spain in 1865. The even grey background of certain works reveals his admiration for Goya. In 1861, he exhibited at the Salon (**The Spanish Singer,** New York, Metropolitan Museum); in 1863, his **Lunch on the Grass** was refused by the jury with two other canvases and was exhibited at the "Salon of the Rejected," where it caused a scandal. Several private exhibitions of his work were held at the Martinet Gallery (1861, 1863, 1865), and in 1867—the year of the Universal Exhibition—he showed the works refused by the official jury in a pavilion at the Alma. At about the same time, he took part in the meetings at the café Guerbois where he met the Naturalist painters and writers. He commanded the respect of the young painters and became the centre of the group which founded Impressionism, yet he never exhibited with them. He became a staff-officer of the National Guard

Manet

Stem of peonies
and secateurs. 1864.

Peonies in a vase
on a small pedestal. 1864.

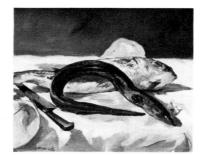

Eel and red-mullet. 1864.

Angelina. 1865.

●□ A bullfight. 1865-66.
(See frontispiece.)

The fife. 1866.

in 1870 and after the war, went with his family to Oloron, Arcachon and Bordeaux, where he painted landscapes. It was then he began the open-air painting to which he devoted himself in the following years under the influence of Monet, whom he had met again in Argenteuil. He became ill with ataxy in 1880. He made stays in Bellevue (1880), Versailles (1881) and Rueil (1882), where he executed a series of views of gardens. From 1863 on, Manet regularly sent his works to the official Salons, where they were frequently refused (1866 and 1867, then in 1876). Nor were they understood by a public rendered cautions by the scandal of **Olympia** (1865).

Emile Zola. 1868.

Reading. 1868.

Madame Manet at the piano. 1868.

The balcony. 1868-69.

Moonlight over the harbour
at Boulogne. 1869.

Berthe Morisot with a fan. 1872.

Woman with fans. 1873.

Manet

●□ On the beach. 1873.

Marguerite de Conflans. 1875-77.

Madame Manet on a blue sofa. 1874-78.

Stephane Mallarmé. 1876.

Blond woman with bare breasts.
1878.

Waitress with beer-glasses.
1878-79.

Georges Clemenceau. 1879.

Manet

Madame Emile Zola. 1879-80.

Doctor Materne. 1880.

Asparagus. 1880.

Lemon. 1880.

Pinks and clematis
in a crystal vase. 1882.

Manet

Olympia.

In 1865, partly because of encouragement from Baudelaire who admired the painting, Manet decided to exhibit his **Olympia** at the Salon. This large canvas had been executed in 1863, in the same year in which Manet had presented his **Lunch on the Grass,** and had been violently attacked by the official critics and the usual public of the Salon. Yet **Olympia** is certainly one of the artist's most important works, since in sets him definitively apart from academic tendencies and shows him to be at the source of modern painting, in which the pictural organisation of the painted surface takes precedence over the subject.

The theme was indeed in the tradition of Titian's famous **Venus** or Goya's **Majas,** but the public of the period sneered at such unusual features as the black cat and the black servant. However, it was the style of the painting even more than the subject which shocked spectators used to the china-smooth surfaces and bland colours of Cabanel's **Birth of Venus,** which had just been bought by the Emperor Napoleon III.

Olympia is painted in frankly contrasting colours, remniscent of the clear-cut forms in the Japanese prints Manet admired; the simple modelling, the wide, vigourous brush-strokes, were contrary to the principles taught at the Academy: yet this picture was to serve as a model for the young painters in revolt against official art—the *Impressionists.* **Olympia** remained, unbought, in the artist's studio and was acquired by his widow in 1890, thanks to a public subscription organised by Claude Monet, then presented to the Luxembourg Museum.

It was also thanks to Monet, with encouragement from Clemenceau, that **Olympia** was finally exhibited in 1907 in the Louvre, in the States Room, opposite Ingres's **Great Odalisk,** thus symbolising Manet's official consecration.

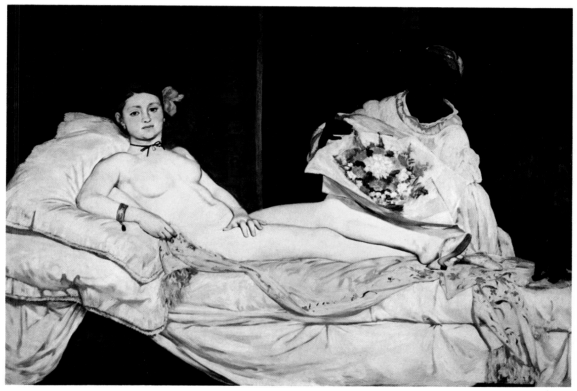

Olympia.

Monet

Claude
1840-1926

Interior of a studio. 1861.

Hunt trophy. 1862.

Still-life. 1864.

Farmyard in Normandy. 1864.

The Pavé de Chailly. 1865.

The cart. Road under snow at Honfleur. 1867.

Born in Paris, spent his youth at Le Havre where Boudin initiated him in open-air painting. In 1859, he worked at the Académie Suisse in Paris, where he met Pissarro. In 1860, he met Jongkind at Le Havre. In 1862, he joined Gleyre's studio in Paris and there became friendly with Renoir, Sisley and Bazille. They painted together from nature in the Forest of Fontainebleau. Monet exhibited for the first time at the 1865 Salon. Until 1870, he lived either in Normandy or in the Parisian region. His work at this period reveals the influence of Courbet and Manet, but **Women in the Garden,** executed in 1867, shows he was making new experiments and evolving towards a light palette and open-air painting. During the war, he went with Pissarro to England, where he admired the works of Turner, then returned by way of Holland and lived in Argenteuil from 1872 to 1878. Monet participated in most of the group's exhibitions and held his first one-man show in 1880. In Véthueil (1878-1883) he became increasingly absorbed in studies of light and atmosphere and these led, during the Giverny period (1883 till his death) to the famous *Series* from which he eliminated everything but the pure study of the vibrations of light (**Haystacks,** 1891; **Poplars,** 1890-91; **Cathedrals of Rouen,** 1892-94; **Water-lilies,** from 1899 on). His various

Fragment
of "Lunch
on the Grass."
1865-66.

Garden in flower. 1866.

Women in the garden. 1867.

Madame Gaudibert. 1868.

High sea at Etretat. 1868.

A country train. 1870-71.

Hôtel des Roches Noires,
Trouville. 1870.

travels in Normandy (Pourville 1882, Etretat, 1883 and 1885), on the Riviera (1884 and 1888), in Britanny (Belle-Ile, 1886), England (from 1899 on), and Italy (Venice, 1908) provided him with a great variety of armospheres for his motifs.

During the war, in Giverny, he started to make numerous large studies of **Water-lilies,** intended for a decoration which he offered to the State in 1822, but at which he continued to work until his death. The panels were placed, according to his wish, in the two rooms of the Orangery of the Tuileries. It is in the work of Monet that we see the most perfect expression of Impressionism.

Monet

Fish-cart at anchor. 1871.

Madame Monet on the sofa. 1871.

Zaandam. 1871.

Landscape. View of plain at Argenteuil. 1872.

Quarries. Saint-Denis. 1872.

Argenteuil. 1872.

●□ Regatta at Argenteuil. 1872.

The brook at Robec. 1872.

Wild poppies. 1873.

The Seine at Argenteuil. 1873.

Resting under the lilacs. 1873.

Monet

The railway bridge at Argenteuil. 1873.

Pleasure-boats. 1873.

The lunch. 1873.

The bridge at Argenteuil. 1874.

Boats. Regatta at Argenteuil. 1874.

The dock at Argenteuil. 1875.

The Tuileries. 1875.

Interior of an apartment. 1875.

Gare Saint-Lazare. 1877.

Monet

Turkey-cocks. 1877.

The church at Vétheuil. 1879.

Camille on her death-bed. 1879.

Chrysanthemums. 1878.

The Seine at Vétheuil.
Sun effect after the rain. 1879.

Break-up on the Seine. 1880.

The church at Vétheuil. Snow. 1878-79.

Landscape. Vétheuil. 1879.

The Seine at Vétheuil. 1879-82.

Hoar-frost. 1880.

Monet

Etretat. 1883.

The Seine at Port-Villez. 1883.

Storm on the Belle-Ile coast. 1886.

Tulip-field in Holland. 1886.

Boat at Giverny. 1887.

●□ Haystacks. 1891.

□ Woman with parasol
turned left. 1886.

Woman with parasol
turned right. 1886.

Rocks at Belle-Ile. 1886.

Rouen Cathedral.
The portal and the Saint-Romain
tower, full sun. Harmony in blue
and gold. 1894.

Monet

Harmony in blue.

Monet made another journey to London in 1891 and went once more to see Turner's works. He did not really like them, but they influenced him profoundly. On his return, he began to paint numerous *series,* which were quickly bought by eager connaisseurs. **Haystacks** and **Poplars** were pretexts for reproducing on canvas a succession of visual instants. He wrote to Geoffrey, "I'm working like mad, trying to capture a series of differing impressions... the further I go, the more I see what a tremendous lot of work it takes to render what I am seeking for, "instantaneity," the outer envelope of things, the same light cast over everything, and I am more disgusted than ever with things come easily, at a first attempt. In fact, I am crazier than ever with the need to reproduce what I feel..."

In 1892, he set up his easel in front of the cathedral of Rouen, so as to make studies whenever he wished of this décor which he transformed according to the varying light or different times of day. Sometimes the portal or the Tower of St. Romain gleams in a vibrant sun with wide blue shadows; sometimes it is blurred in a late afternoon mist, so that the architecture seems to exist only in order to support or reflect this mist. Harmony in blue, harmony in brown... these **Cathedrals** are as varied as if the subject was different in each painting.

The series of twenty canvases representing **Cathedrals** was finished in 1894 and exhibited the following year in Durand-Ruel's gallery, where they had a great success. Comte Isaac de Camondo chose four of them, which were among the collection he left to the Louvre. In 1907, the Luxembourg Museum bought a **Cathedral,** a harmony in brown, which was the only painting of this artist, together with **Women in the Garden,** bought by the state.

Harmony in blue.

Monet

Rouen Cathedral.
The portal and the
Saint-Romain tower.
Morning study.
Harmony in white. 1894.

● Rouen Cathedral.
The portal. Morning sun.
Harmony in blue. 1894.

Rouen Cathedral.
The portal. Cloudy weather.
1894.

Rouen Cathedral.
Harmony in brown. 1894.

Mount Kolsaas, in Norway. 1895.

A branch of the Seine, near Giverny. 1897.

The water-lily pond.
Harmony in green. 1899.

●□ The water-lily pond.
Harmony in green. 1899.

Vétheuil. Setting sun. 1901.

London. The Parliament. 1904.

Self-portrait. 1917.

Morisot

Berthe
1841-1895

The butterfly catchers. 1874.

●The cradle. 1872.

In the cornfield. 1875.

Young woman powdering her face. 1877.

Young woman dressed for the ball. 1879.

Louise Riesener. 1888.

Hydrangea. 1894.

The children of Gabriel Thomas. 1894.

Berthe Morisot showed an early talent for painting. She worked with with Chocard, then with Guichard, a native of Lyons, who had been a pupil of Ingres and Delacroix. In 1860 she was painting in the open-air with Corot. However, the most important influence in her life was Manet, whom she met in the Louvre in 1868, when she was copying from Rubens. After spending a holiday in Fécamp, where the Manet and Morisot families were staying, she agreed to marry Eugène Manet, the painter's brother, in December 1874. During their engagement, Edouard Manet made several portraits of his future sister-in-law, one of which, **Berthe Morisot with a Fan,** came to the Louvre with the Moreau-Nélaton collection. A few years earlier, she had been the model for one of the figures of Manet's **Balcony.** In 1874, she took part in the first Impressionist exhibition and thereafter exhibited regularly with the group. From 1880 on, her work shows the influence of Renoir, specially in the more varied palette.

Morisot

The Cradle.

Berthe Morisot was the only woman painter who took part, together with Degas, Monet, Renoir, Sisley, Pissarro, Cézanne and Guillaumin, in the first exhibition of their works, held in Nadar's studio. It was here that **The Cradle** was shown for the first time.

The work is said to have been inspired by the sight of her sister, Edma Pontillon, watching her new-born baby as it slept. Berthe Morisot often stayed with her sister at Maurecourt, where she also painted her playing with her children in **The Butterfly Hunt,** now in the Jeu de Paume. The classical simplicity of Berthe Morisot's work caused less scandal among the public, and at the sale of Impressionist works held in 1875, it was she who fetched the highest prices.

The Cradle is one of Berthe Morisot's greatest successes. It reveals delicate craftsmanship and feminine sensibility, but there is no trace of maukishness in the grouping and composition. Everything here is subtle and harmonious. The light veiling bordered with pink, contrasts with the milky whiteness of sheets tinged here and there with blue. The head of the sleeping child is coloured with the lightest of touches. The ensemble is truly enchanting. Paul Valéry defined the artist in the following terms. "Berthe Morisot stands apart because she lived her painting and painted her life, as if painting was for her a natural and necessary function." The canvas remained in the family of the artist's sister and was acquired by the Museum in 1930.

The cradle.

Pissarro

Camille
1830-1903

Landscape at Montmorency. 1859.

The ferry-boat at La Varenne-Saint-Hilaire. 1864.

The Louveciennes road. 1870.

The country-cottage. The pink house. 1870.

The coach at Louveciennes. 1870.

Winter landscape at Louveciennes. 1870.

He came to study in Paris (1842-1847) then returned to the West Indies, became friendly with the Danish painter Fritz Melbye, and worked in Venezuela. He returned to Paris in 1885, where he worked for short periods in the studios, making the acquaintance of Claude Monet at the Académie Suisse. He painted in the open air and was influenced by Delacroix, Courbet and above all Corot. He exhibited at the Salon of the Rejected in 1863 and at the official salons in 1864-65-66. Until the war, he lived at Pontoise, then at Louveciennes. In 1870, he went, like Monet, to England. After his return, he took part regularly in all the Impressionist manifestations.

Having settled once more in Pontoise, he brought Cézanne there and initiated him in open-air painting and the use of a light palette. Soon after, he began to be influenced in his turn by the Master from Aix.

Unlike Claude Monet, he seldom painted water and its changing reflections. He was to be the interpreter of the earth, and country landscapes. In 1884, he settled definitively at Eragny, where he joined the Neo-Impressionist movement under the influence of Seurat (1886-88), before returning to his original technique. Frequent journeys towards the end of his life and numerous views of cities (Paris, Rouen).

Pissarro

Harvest at Montfoucault

It was while he was staying with Ludovic Piette at Montfoucault, his country home at Melleraye in the Mayenne, that Pissarro painted **The Harvest** and other studies of the fields surrounding his friend's estate.

Cézanne was painting at the time in the port of l'Estaque, yet his influence on Pissarro is evident in this canvas. The technique is broad and strong, and the volumes are produced by means of masses with colourful shadows. The green of trees and bushes thus becomes dense and luminous. The occasional figures, touched in with red and blue, are there to provide counterpoints completing the harmony of the ensemble.

Pissarro was also interested in portrait-painting. He was one of the few landscape painters in the group who introduced human figures into views of the country—peasants in the style of Millet, busy at their daily work, a sower or a plower, painted this same year at Montfoucault.

Pissarro was fortunate in that he was at the origin of the evolution of geniuses such as Cézanne and Seurat, so that he saw his own ideas being transformed by men with talent more powerful than his own, and came in his turn under their influence.

The Harvest was bought almost immediately by Caillebotte, together with other canvases painted at Montfoucault, which were refused by the State when it came into the Caillebotte bequest in 1894.

Harvest at Montfoucault.

Pissarro

Hillsides at Le Vésinet. 1871.

The wash-house. Pontoise. 1872.

The Louveciennes road. 1872.

Pontoise. 1872.

Entrance to the village at Voisins. 1872.

Chestnut-trees at Louveciennes. 1872.

Self-portrait. 1873.

Hoarfrost. 1873.

The Ennery road near Pontoise. 1874.

...ndscape. Pontoise. 1875.

● Harvest at Montfoucault. 1876.

The coach. The Ennery road
at l'Hermitage. 1877.

□ Red roofs. 1877.

Undergrowth, in summer. 1877.

Kitchen-garden and trees in blossom. In spring.
Pontoise. 1877.

A garden plot at l'Hermitage.
1877.

By the Oise river, near Pontoise.
Cloudy weather. 1878.

Uphill road across country. 1879.

Pissarro

Kitchen-garden at l'Hermitage. 1879.

Landscape at Chaponval. 1880.

The wheelbarrow. 1881.

●□ Girl with a stick. 1881.

Woman hanging out washing. 1887.

Woman in a close. Eragny. 1887.

Woman with green kerchief. 1893.

The church at Knocke. 1894.

Snow effect at Eragny. 1894.

Pissarro

Landscape at Eragny. 1895.

The harbour at Rouen. Saint-Sever. 1896.

Woman in an orchard. Eragny. 1897.

The wash-house at Bazincourt. 1900.

Saint-Jacques Church at Dieppe. 1901.

Dieppe, Dusquesne Dock. 1902.

Moret. The Loing canal. 1902.

The Seine and the Louvre. 1903.

Redon

Odilon
1840-1916

Madame Odilon Redon. 1882.

Flowers in a vase:
the red poppy.

Closed eyes. 1890.

Flowers.

Paul Gauguin. 1903-1905.

After working for a short time in Gérôme's studio, Odilon Redon, who spent his time between Bordeaux and Paris, fell under the influence of the engraver Rodolphe Bresdin, who communicated to him his admiration for Rembrandt. Redon worked on his own, but was in touch with Chintreuil, Courbet, Corot, etc. After the 1870 war, he settled in Paris and executed numerous lithographies on the advice of Fantin-Latour. He exhibited at the Salon des Independants in 1884, but participated nevertheless with Gauguin in the eighth and last Impressionist exhibition in 1886. He exhibited in Durand-Ruel and Vollard's galleries from 1895 and travelled frequently in Belgium, Italy, Holland and Spain. Redon, who was a friend of the Symbolists, Mallarmé and musicians like Ernest Chausson, interprets the secret universe of Being with a rare feeling for line and colour.

Renoir

Pierre-Auguste
1841-1919

William Sisley. 1864.

Frédéric Bazille. 1867.

Madame Théodore Charpentier. 1869.

Lighters on the Seine. 1869.

Reclining half-nude woman. 1872.

The Seine at Argenteuil. 1873.

Renoir started by painting on china and hoped to work for the Sèvres Manufactury. He was admitted to the School of Fine Arts in 1862 and entered Gleyre's studio, where he met Sisley, Bazille and Claude Monet. They painted together from nature in the Forest of Fontainebleau. From 1864, he exhibited almost every year at the Salon and took part in the first Impressionist Exhibition in 1874, but abandoned the exhibitions of the group several times to return to the official Salon. His early works reveals the influence of Diaz and, briefly, that of Courbet, but above all that of Delacroix. After 1872, he adopted Impressionist technique under the influence of Monet and applied it to the interpretation of figures in open-air—portaits of a single model or scenes with several figures, evoking the joy of living. Renoir returned with vividly coloured canvases from his two journeys to Algeria in 1881 and 1882.

The study of Ingres and a journey to Italy (1881-82) brought the revelation of Raphael and the Primitives and led him in about 1883 to lose interest in Impressionism. This was his "Ingresque" period, characterised by precise drawing, chilly treatment and acid colouring. Renoir travelled a great deal, staying on the Normandy coast, in Guernsey, the Riviera (1883) and La Rochelle (1884).

Madame Darras. 1873.

Woman reading. 1874.

Charles Le Cœur. 1874.

Portrait of a woman,
also known as Madame
Georges Hartmann. 1874.

Claude Monet. 1875.

Young woman
with a hat-veil. 1875.

Young woman
sitting in a garden. 1875.

From 1885, the artist divided his time between Paris and Essoyes, near Troyes, his wife's birthplace.
Towards 1890, Renoir readopted a less precise treatment. Renouncing modern subjects, he painted chiefly portraits and nudes, the latter becoming more and more numerous as time went on. Towards 1892, he travelled both in France and abroad (England, Holland) then, in 1903, he settled in Cagnes, where he was to spend the rest of his life. He continued to paint, in spite of illness and suffering, producing works in which red is the dominant colour, expressive of the lyricism he reveals constantly, but which is to be seen at its most intense in his last manner.

Renoir

Torso of a woman in the sun. 1876.

● The Moulin de la Galette. 1876.

By the Seine at Champrosay. 1876.

Madame Alphonse Daudet. 1876.

The swing. 1876.

●□ Path through tall grass. 1876-77.

Madame Georges Charpentier. 1876-77.

●□ Portrait of Margot. 1878.

Renoir

Le Moulin de la Galette.

This large composition is said to have been painted in the open-air. Each evening, Renoir brought his canvas back to a studio he rented nearby in the rue Cortot. It was probably a smaller study which the artist transported in this way and which he used when he was painting his large picture. This study, with several variations, is now in the John Hay Whitney collection in New York.

Renoir had been enchanted by the rustic spot on the Butte Montmartre where the Moulin de la Galette stood in a lucern field. On Sundays, people came to dance and eat girdle-cakes ("galettes") from three o'clock till nightfall. Painters came to seek for models among the little girls of the quarter, who, Rivière tells us, used to "escape in secret from their mothers' homes to dance the polka or show off a summer dress."

Renoir used his friends as models: "Estelle, Jeanne's sister, who can be seen on the bench in the foreground, Lamy, Norbert Goeneutte, the painter Georges Rivière seated at a table, Gervex, Cordey, Lestringuez, Lhote among the dancers. A painter from Cuba in the centre of the picture, wearing gosling green trousers, is dancing with Margot."

All the charm of this composition lies in the play of light shining on or shading the faces as it infiltrates the thin foliage of the trees. This flickering and shimmering of colours and shadows, creates an atmosphere of intense life, of joy and youth.

Caillebotte bought this picture, chiefly to help Renoir, at the 1877 exhibition. Vollard tells us that Caillebotte had expressed the wish that after his death Renoir should choose a picture from his collection. The time came just at the moment when Renoir had learned that a connaisseur was prepared to pay 50,000 F for **Le Moulin de la Galette** and accordingly made it his choice. The Caillebotte family, however, refused to give up one of the most important among the paintings destined for the Luxembourg Museum. Renoir therefore chose a Degas.

The Moulin de la Galette.

Renoir

Madame Paul Bérard.
1879.

Self-portrait. 1879.

Alphonsine Fournaise. 1879.

Portrait of a woman. 1880.

The railway bridge at Chatou. 1881.

Richard Wagner. 1882.

Algerian landscape. 1881.

An Arab feast at Algers. 1881.

Banana-fields. 1881.

Dance in the city. 1883.

Seascape-Guernsey. 1883.

Sword-lilies. 1885.

Still-life.

Woman drawing water.

Half-length nude. 1886.

Moss-roses. 1890.

Roses in a vase. 1890.

Young girls at the piano. 1892.

Renoir

Reader in green. 1894.

Nude. Unfinished study.
1895.

Madame Gaston Bernheim
de Villers. 1901.

●□ Ode to flowers. 1903-09.

The toilet: woman combing
her hair. 1907-08.

Little girl with
a straw hat. 1908.

Reclining nude, seen from the back. 1909.

Young girl seated. 1909.

Monsieur et Madame Bernheim
de Villers. 1910.

Renoir

Geneviève Bernheim de Villers.
1910.

Gabrielle with a rose. 1911.

Young woman with a rose. 1913.

In a garden. 1911-15.

Reader in white. 1915-16.

Odalisque sleeping. 1915-17.

● Women bathing. 1918-19.

Landscape.

The great judgement of Pâris. 1914.

Renoir

Women bathing.

Towards the end of his life, Renoir made increasing use of a warm red, slightly tinged with mauve. In his retreat in the Villa des Collettes in Cagnes, crippled with rheumatism and paralysed, he worked furiously on. He executed several large compositions, such as these **Women Bathing.** Instead of projecting his subject directly on the canvas he made small preliminary studies in red chalk. Then he traced the composition onto the canvas by means of a reddish-brown pastel.

These bathers are Ruben's women, transported into the luxuriant gardens of the South. They have become part of the vegetation. Like it, they are gorged with sun, they flower and spread, radiating heat and life. Renoir, who felt his own life growing feebler and whose activity was limited by his infirmities, put all his hopeless longing for strength and vitality into his painting. This violent lyricism, which appears so joyful and expresses itself in rapturous colour, is akin to Van Gogh's despairing lyricism. "It is now that I have neither legs nor arms," said Renoir, "That I long to paint large canvases. I dream of nothing but Veronese, of the **Wedding at Caana.** What misery!" It was this picture by the Venetian master which he came in his wheel-chair to see in the Louvre, shortly before his death.

The picture was in the studio at the Villa des Collettes when he died. The painter's son offered it to the Louvre in 1923, refusing a very tempting offer from the American collector Barnes.

The canvas was first shown in the Luxembourg Museum (the Museum of Modern Art of the period) before being exhibited in the Louvre in 1929.

Women bathings

Rousseau

●War. 1894.

Portrait of a woman.
1895-97.

□ The snake-charmer. 1907.

His father was an ironmonger in Laval. It is possible that he took part as a musician, between the ages of 18 and 23, in the Mexican campaign. He served as a sergeant in the war of 1870. After the defeat, he was employed for thirteen years at the Paris city toll. He retired at forty and began to paint, while earning his living in various small jobs—copying records, working as sales inspector for the *Petit Parisien*, as shopkeeper, or teacher of drawing or music. He married twice. He exhibited at the Salon des Indépendants and the Salon d'Automne. Pissarro and Gauguin were interested in his painting; it amused Jarry and aroused enthusiasm in Apollinaire. His friends and admirers often met at his home and they organised a great banquet in his honour. He died at the Necker hospital on 2 September 1910.

He was an amateur painter, depicting the suburbs and people of Paris, but he is also a painter of allegories and of a Mexico transfigured by his imagination. His technique is naif yet extraordinarily daring, uniting delicate colouring with the monumental rhythm of a great decorative artist.

Rousseau

War.

In 1893, Henri Rousseau, an employee of the Paris toll-house, retired and decided to devote himself exclusively to painting. At that date he had already exhibited at the Salon des Indépendants; Pissarro had admired the amazing exuberance and sincerity of his work. Yet Rousseau had no connection with Impressionism and considered the very official Gerôme as one of his masters. Though he was entirely self-taught, he invented a technique which enabled him to express himself as he desired. **War** or **The Ride of Discord** was shown at the Salon des Indépendants in 1894 and was described in the catalogue: "War (its horrifying passage, leaving despair, tears and ruin everywhere)." In 1895, Rémy de Gourmont published in his review **l'Ymagier** the only know lithograph of the Douanier Rousseau. Its theme and composition are the same as that of the painting.

The various elements of the picture—the horse, the heaped corpses in a strange dawn light—are depicted with hallucinating precision; yet this funereal allegory is transfigured by the beauty of the colours and we are struck above all by the extraordinary imagination which inspired it.

The artist's ingenuous vision bears in fact the evident imprint of a conscious mental process without which these forms could never have been interpreted with such unerring sureness. The Douanier Rousseau thus counts among the painters of the end of the 19th century who opened the way for novel aesthetic theories concerning the liberty of the artist to create forms. Thus Gauguin, and later Picasso, understood and appreciated his work. Rousseau is a great master who cannot easily be defined. His works are the mysterious echo of his mysterious originality.

War

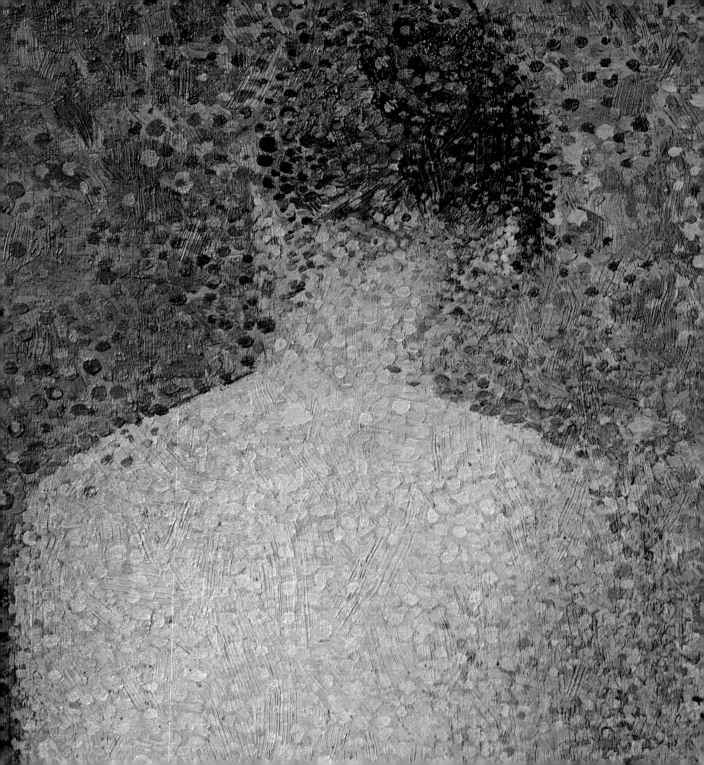

Seurat

Georges-Pierre
1859-1891

Outskirts of a forest in spring. 1882-83.

Study for bathing at Asnières. 1883.

Study for Sunday afternoon
at the Ile de la Grande Jatte. 1884.

Study for Sunday afternoon
at the Ile de la Grande Jatte. 1884.

Pink landscape. 1882-84.

THESE WORKS ARE SHOWN IN THE EXHIBITION, POST-IMPRESSIONISM, AT THE PALAIS DE TOKYO.

During his years at the School of Fine Arts, Seurat became imbued with classical culture and with the example of Ingres. At the same time, he became interested in Delacroix's principles of the harmony of colours and studied the scientific theories of physicists like Chevreuil concerning light. This led him to reduce his palette to four basic colours: red, blue, yellow and green and their intermediate tones. Instead of mixing these colours directly one with the other, the painter juxtaposed small blobs of pure colour, with the result that these blended optically in the eye of the spectator. Seurat named this method *divisionism*.

In 1884, his first large picture, **The Bathing Place** (London, National Gallery) was refused for the Salon, whereupon he founded the Salon des Indépendants with Signac and Redon. He became the leader of the Neo-Impression group which included Signac, Cross, Pissarro for a moment, Luce, etc.

In 1886, his admirable **Sunday Afternoon at the Ile de La Grande Jatte** (Chicago, Art Institute) was shown at the eighth and last Impressionist exhibition, where it was sneered at by the critics.

Seurat died young, leaving unfinished a canvas exhibited at the Salon des Indépendants, **The Circus**.

Seurat

The Circus.

In this scene, for which he made several studies at Fernando's Circus, Seurat concentrated on contrasts, comparing the curving lines of the ring, the movement of the horse and the equestrienne, with the vertical immobility of the spectators. He also contrasts the red of the clown, intersecting the composition in the foreground, with his blueish shadow, which is scattered so as to blend gradually with the orange-yellow of the ring. Seurat was applying here his theory of methodical fragmentation in the application of the paint (divisionism and pointillism). Optical blending is substituted for the blend of pigments, thus obtaining far greater luminosity.

Before painting his large compositions, Seurat made numerous studies from life, which he called **croquetons,** and these enabled him to work afterwards in his studio. There exists a small sketch for **The Circus** (R.F. 1937-123).

The picture remained unfinished. Signac said of the painter's death that "a sort of luminous apparition, his **Circus,** his dream of colours... must have appeared to him as he lay dying." The canvas was on show, at the moment of his death, at the Salon des Indépendants.

Signac bought **The Circus** in 1900 and later it became part of the John Quinn collection. Signac was distressed to think that yet another of Seurat's works would go abroad and he suggested to the collector that he might leave it to the Louvre after his death. **The Circus** was thus bequeathed to the Louvre in 1927.

The Circus

Seurat

Model in profile. 1887.

Model in full-face. 1887.

●□ Model from the back.
1887.

Port-en-Bessin. Outer-harbour, high tide.
1888.

● The Circus. 1891.

Sketch for The Circus. 1891.

Signac

Paul
1863-1935

Outskirts of Paris. 1883.

By the river. The Seine at Herblay. 1889.

The green sail. Venice. 1904.

The red buoy. 1895.

Woman reading
by lamp-light. 1890.

THESE WORKS ARE SHOWN IN THE EXHIBITION, POST-IMPRESSIONISM, AT THE PALAIS DE TOKYO.

Paul Signac joined the Impressionists very early in his career, but when he saw Seurat's first canvases, he did not hesitate to participate in this new movement, which seemed revolutionary at the time. He persuaded Pissarro, whom he had met in 1885 at Guillaumin's home, to join it.

The Neo-Impressionist theories exactly suited Signac, who was a great lover of the sea. Never, perhaps, has the density of calm water and the reality of its luminosity, been rendered with greater feeling.

Signac was anxious to preserve the documents concerning his various travels and made numerous water-colour sketches, painting with rapid, vibrant brush-strokes.

Sisley

Alfred
1839-1899

Heron with spread wings. 1865-67.

View of Saint-Martin canal. 1870.

Resting by the brook. 1872.

The foot-bridge at Argenteuil. 1872.

Saint-Martin canal. 1872.

Rue de la Chaussée at Argenteuil. 1872.

Sisley was of British nationality and had come with his parents to live in France. He hoped to obtain French naturalisation but was never able to do so. In 1862, he worked in Gleyre's studio, where he met Monet, Renoir and Bazille. His early work was influenced by Corot, Courbat and Daubigny. He painted at Marlotte (1866), stayed in Honfleur (1867), then in Bougival and Louveciennes. From 1870, he came under the influence of Monet and painted landscapes of the Ile-de-France (Voisins, Marly). After making a journey to England, he lived in Sèvres from 1875 to 1879 and settled definitively in Moret in 1882. He took part in the Impressionist exhibitions of 1874-76-77-82 and was refused by the Salon in 1879. Durand-Ruel gave him a one-man show in 1883. In 1884, he went to Rouen and in 1897 made a short stay in England. He was the most unfortunate of all the Impressionists and remained all his life unknown or despised. His success began a few weeks after his death, due perhaps to articles by Gustave Geffroy.

Sisley

The Ile Saint-Denis. 1872.

The Ile de la Grande-Jatte. 1873.

The Seine at Bougival. 1873.

Boats at the Bougival lock. 1873.

The road, view of the Sèvres road. 1873.

Louveciennes. Hill-tops at Marly. 1873.

Regatta at Molesey. 1874.

Fog. 1874.

The village of Voisins. 1874.

Snow at Marly-le-Roi. 1875.

The forge at Marly-le-Roi. 1875.

The Versailles road. 1875.

●Boat in the flood at Port-Marly. 1876.

The flood at Port-Marly. 1876.

In the snow. A farm yard at Marly-le-Roi.
1876.

●□ The Seine at Suresnes. 1877.

The Louveciennes road. 1877-78.

Sisley

Boat in the Flood at Port-Marly.

Sisley was of British nationality and had settled in Paris with his parents. He met Monet, Renoir and Bazille at Gleyre's studio and gradually freed himself under their influence from that of Corot, Courbet and Daubigny. On his return from England, he worked at Louveciennes and Marly, seeking like his Impressionist friends to represent things in their own surroundings and produce an impression of reality. He explained his ideas to Tavernier, who owned another version of this picture which came to the Louvre at the same time through the Camondo collection: "The subject, the motif, must always be translated in a simple, understandable way which grips the spectator. Elimination of superfluous details will lead the latter to follow the painter's suggestions and see first of all what it was that excited him. There must always be movement somewhere in the picture. That is part of the charm of Corot, and of Jongkind too. Next to the subject, one of the most interesting qualities in a landscape is life and movement. It is also one of the hardest to reproduce. Everything must contribute to it—form, colour, treatment. It is the painter's emotion which confers life and this emotion arouses that of the spectator."

All the Impressionists, and especially Sisley, were attracted by the motif of calm water. In this picture, Sisley uses Corot's technique for the pinkish walls of the house and for the trees, and that of Monet in the reflections on the water, painted with wide, superimposed brush-strokes which give a vibrant effect. Sisley was the most unfortunate of the group. He remained misunderstood and despised for a long time. The attention of the public was drawn to him through an article by Geoffroy published after his death.

Boat in the flood at Port-Marly.

Sisley

Snow at Louveciennes. 1878.

Rainy spring in the outskirts of Paris. 1879.

Snow at Veneux-Nadon. 1880.

Skirt of a forest in spring. 1880.

The Seine from the hillside of By. 1881.

Edge of a wood at the Sablons. 1883.

Farmyard at Saint-Mammès. 1884.

The Loing canal. 1884.

Saint-Mammès. 1885.

Aspens and acacias. 1889.

Moret, by the Loing river. 1892.

The Loing canal. 1892.

The bridge at Moret. 1893.

Toulouse-Lautrec

Henri de
1864-1901

Henry Samary. 1889.

Woman combing her hair. 1891.

Justine Dieuhl. 1891.

Woman with gloves. 1891.

Woman with a black feather boa.
1892.

●□ In bed. 1892.

Toulouse-Lautrec was a direct descendant of the Counts of Toulouse, coming from a very ancient family in which there had been a certain number of artists and excentrics. In about his fifteenth year he broke both legs, one after the other, and remained crippled. He was a student of Princeteau and an admirer of John-Lewis Brown. He began his career with brilliant studies of horses and rustic scenes. Then, under the influence of Degas, he began to take an interest in contemporary life, studying it chiefly in the places of amusement and the night life in which he found a refuge. At the same time he discovered in Japanese prints the beauty of arabesques and the supple, condensed lines he used in his paintings, engravings and posters.

In 1886, he met in Cormon's studio a young painter newly arrived in Paris, Vincent Van Gogh, and for several months the two artists influenced each other mutually. Toulouse-Lautrec's health was ruined by drink and he was interned for several months in 1899. He left the clinic of Neuilly-sur-Seine only to die in 1901 in his family castle at Malromé.

Toulouse-Lautrec

Jane Avril Dancing.

It was during an evening spent at the Moulin Rouge in 1892 that Toulouse-Lautrec sketched in a few lines the strange silhouette of Jane Avril, a dancer who had become famous under the name of "La mélinite." In the middle ground we see, in profile, a woman and Mr. Warner, an impresario who was the model for a well-known lithograph by this artist: **Englishman at the Moulin Rouge** (1892). Toulouse-Lautrec admired the graceful Jane Avril, who was slim and dressed with a refined elegance and whose melancholy expression contrasted with the noisy vulgarity of "La Goulue," whom he also immortalised.

Toulouse-Lautrec's art owes much to Degas, both in the choice of subjects taken from the theatre or music-hall, and in its underlying conception. It was through Degas that Lautrec discovered the possibilities in Japanese prints. Paradoxically, it was in the studio of Cormon, the most academic of painters, that Lautrec had met Emile Bernard and discovered his vocation. It was there too that in 1886, he met a young artist recently arrived in Paris, Van Gogh, and for several months the two painters influenced each other mutually. From that time on, Lautrec went beyond Impressionist experiments and developed a highly personal style, the terse incisive delineation of his portraits often bordering on caricature. The audacity of his aesthetic methods is also revealed in his lithographs. He is a pioneer in this field and his influence revolutionised poster art.

Jane Avril dancing.

Toulouse-Lautrec

● Jane Avril dancing.
1892.

Woman pulling up her stocking.
1894.

Blond woman from a brothel.
1894.

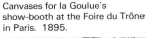

Canvases for la Goulue's
show-booth at the Foire du Trône
in Paris. 1895.

The Moresque dance,
also called Les Almées Dance
at the Moulin-Rouge.

The clowness Cha-U-Kao. 1895.

Profile of a woman. 1896.

Dance at the Moulin-Rouge
(La Goulue and Valentin le Désossé).

●□ Woman at her toilet. 1896.

Paul Leclercq. 1897.

Louis Bouglé. 1898.

Van Gogh

Vincent
1853-1890

Head of a peasant woman from Holland. 1884.

Fritillaries in a copper vase. 1886.

La guinguette. 1886.

Restaurant de la Sirène at Asnières. 1887.

Italian woman. 1887.

Self-portrait. 1887.

The son of a Dutch minister of religion, he studied theology for a short time and went as minister to the Borinage, in Belgium (1877-78) after having been employed by the art dealer Goupil at The Hague, then in London (1869-76). In 1880 however, he discovered his true vocation as a painter. In his Dutch works he uses sombre tones and heavy brush-strokes to render the oppressive atmosphere among the peasants and weavers he sought to convert (Nuenen period, *The Potato Eaters*, 1885). He came to Paris in 1886, to join his brother Theo, who gave him financial and moral support. This was the time of his encounter with Impressionism and Japanese prints. In 1888 he left Paris for Arles, sending for Gauguin to join him. It soon became evident that the two artists could not live together and after a quarrel, the details of which are not known, Vincent mutilated his ear in an attack of madness. He was admitted at his own request to the Hospice of Saint-Rémy-de-Provence in the Spring of the year 1889. A year later he left Saint-Rémy for Auvers-sur-Oise, home of Dr. Gachet, a specialist in nervous disorders and friend of the Impressionists. On 27 July 1890, Vincent tried to commit suicide and died two days later of his wounds.

Van Gogh

Gypsy encampment with caravans.
1888.

Eugène Boch. 1888.

●□ L'Arlésienne. 1888.

The dance hall in Arles. 1888.

●□ Self-portrait. 1889.

Van Gogh's bedroom at Arles. 1889.

Saint-Jean Hospital in Saint-Rémy.
1889.

□ Noon (after Millet). 1889-90.

Van Gogh

Doctor Gachet's garden
at Auvers-sur-Oise. 1890.

Doctor Paul Gachet. 1890.

Mademoiselle Gachet in her garden.
1890.

● The church at Auvers-sur-Oise.
1890.

Roses and anemones. 1890.

Two little girls. 1890.

Thatched cottages at Cordeville. 1890.

Van Gogh

The Church at Auvers

On 16 May 1890, Van Gogh left the hospice of Saint-Rémy and visited his brother in Paris before leaving for Auvers-sur-Oise. He stayed first at the Saint-Aubin inn, then at the café Ravoux. He took his meals several times a week with Dr. Gachet, who admired his painting and introduced him to engraving techniques. Van Gogh painted his host's garden several times and did his portrait, as well as that of his daughter playing the piano (Bâle Museum).

Van Gogh liked the surrounding landscape. "Auvers is certainly lovely," he said: "I find the modern villas and the country houses of the bourgeoisie nearly as pretty as the old cottages falling into ruin." This isolated countryside was characteristic and picturesque. In June 1890 he described to his sister a picture of the village church he had just painted: "I have treated it in a way which makes the building appear purplish-blue against a sky of deep, simple blue, a pure cobalt; the stained-glass windows make splashes of ultramarine blue, the roof is purple touched with orange. In the foreground there is greenery with flowers and pink sand with the sun on it. It is still almost the same as the studies I made at Nuenen, but the colour is probably more expressive, more sumptuous." Van Gogh had set up his easel behind the church, of which we see the apse. It was restored in 1891, in the year following the artist's death.

This painting belonged to Dr. Gachet and passed to his son Paul. It was acquired by the Louvre thanks to his cooperation and an anonymous donation received from Canada in 1951.

The church at Auvers.

Documentary Panels

1. Techniques

Didactic panels in the documentary room comprise, on the right, details of works shown by means of illuminated ektachromes, and on the left, reproductions of works, with appropriate commentaries, showing the evolution of Impressionist technique.

Pannel I

All the Impressionists aimed, from the start of their researches, to paint in the open air. This led them to seek light, bright colours rendering the impression of brilliant light.

◀ Manet was the first to reject the muddy tones of the Romantics and reduce his palette to a few pure colours.

1

Instead of painting shadow ▶ in neutral greys, the Impressionists attempted to render light entirely by means of colour and even their shadows are coloured.

2

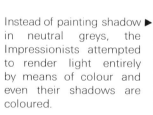

◀ When they painted reflections in moving water, they fragmented their brush-work.

3

Pannel II

By means of increasingly ▶ fragmented brushwork, they obtained an impression of coloured vibration in which the forms are no longer visible.

4

5

A comparison between Millet's **Church at Gréville** and Monet's **Church at Vétheuil** ▶ reveals the novelty of this manner of expressing the quality of the light in such a way that all interpretation of form tends to disappear.

In their paintings, contour and modelling vanish in coloured vibration.

▼

6

◀ Fragmented brush-work led them to break up the tone and attempt to recompose its colours by juxtaposing touches of pure colour which blend in the spectator's eye to produce an impression of vibration, and the sensation of light.

7

Pannel III

The Impressionists took ▶ these discoveries into account and began utilising pure colours instead of mixing them on their palettes.

◀ After reading Chevreul's book (1839) Seurat conceived the idea that the effects produced instinctively by the Impressionists could be obtained methodically. His method has been called Divisionism or Neo-Impressionism.

Pannel IV

In the course of their experiments, they discovered empirically some of the laws concerning the theory of colours, of which Newton had laid the foundations by decomposing sunlight (white light) into its spectral components and reconstituting it by a mixture obtained by adding the colours of the spectrum one to the other. Numerous experiments have in fact shown that:

1. Any colour can be reproduced by blending two or three "primary component" colours.

In painting: small spots of juxtaposed colours viewed from a considerable distance (addition) often blend to produce colours more vivid than those mixed on the palette.

2. Each colour tends to colour its neighbouring space with its complementary colour: law of simultaneous contrasts.

(Two colours are complimentary when, if they are used in the proper quantity and blended by addition, they produce a sensation of pale grey).

Consequence: — if two tones contain a common colour, the latter will be attenuated by juxtaposition;

— two juxtaposed tones will become more vivid.

Precursors and influences

Early in the 19th century, landscape painting in England and subsequently in France freed itself from the intellectualism of the classical school and began to seek a more subtle interpretation of light.

"Grey is the enemy of ▶ all paintings. In nature, everything is reflection."
DELACROIX 1798-1863

"Beauty in art is truth suffused with the impression some aspect of nature has made on us."
COROT 1796-1875

In about 1860, the Dutchman Jongkind and Eugène Boudin were in Le Havre preparing directly for Impressionism by their studies of the coast. "Three brush-strokes from nature are worth more than two days work at the easel." ▶
BOUDIN 1824-1898

◀ Japanese prints were introduced into France about the middle of the century. Young artists discovered in them a new way of looking at the world and were encouraged to break with tradition.
"We specially appreciated the bold manner in which they delimit the subject. These people have taught us to compose our work in a different way, there's no doubt about that."
MONET 1840-1926

▲ Monet and Pissarro were in London in 1870 and were greatly impressed by Turner's landscapes, in which they discovered the same experiments with light and atmosphere they were already making: "the sun is God."
TURNER 1775-1851

Formation of the Group

In about 1862, Renoir, Sisley, Monet and Bazille, Cézanne and Pissarro became acquainted in the Paris *ateliers*, in Gleyre's studio and the Académie Suisse.
1863 - The scandal over **Lunch on the Grass** at the Salon of the Rejected, led these young men to form a group around Manet.
About 1866 - Naturalist painters and writers met at the Café Guerbois and impregnated each other with new ideas.

Dispersal

PARIS
MANET
DEGAS

MONET 1883

1881 SISLEY

GIVERNY

PISSARRO 1884

MORET

VAN GOGH 1888

CÉZANNE 1878

1891 GAUGUIN

ÉRAGNY

1899 RENOIR

TAHITI

ARLES

CAGNES

AIX-EN-PROVENCE

Maturity

After 1872, the Impressionists remained grouped in the region of Paris. This period, during which Impressionist art reached full maturity, is known as the "Argenteuil period."

They held their first exhibition in the studio of the photographer Nadar in 1874. The title of one of Monet's paintings, "Impression, rising sun," earned them the title of Impressionists. They held seven more exhibitions in 1876, 1877, 1879, 1880, 1881, 1882, 1886.

Reactions

1886 - Seurat's "Neo-Impressionism," to which Pissarro adhered until 1888, was an attempt to organise Impressionism scientifically.
1889 - "Symbolism" signified an intellectual reaction which asserted itself when Gauguin, Emile Bernard and Schuffenecker held an exhibition at the café Volpini.

During the 20th century, two new forms of art accentuated the reaction against Impressionism.
1905 - "Fauvism," influenced by Van Gogh and

Gauguin disregarded precise perception in favour of powerful expression.
1908 - "Cubism," stemming from Cézanne, rejected nature in favour of abstract constructions of lines and colours.

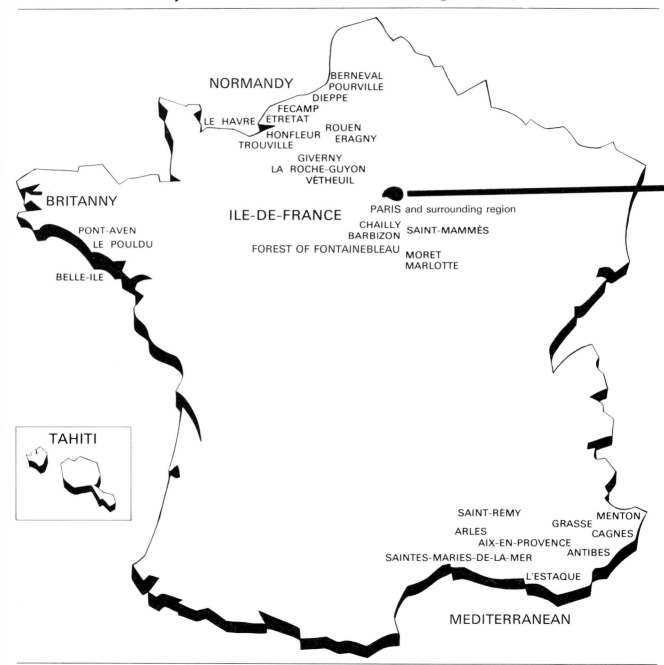

NORMANDY

BERNEVAL
POURVILLE
DIEPPE
FÉCAMP
LE HAVRE ÉTRETAT
ROUEN
HONFLEUR ÉRAGNY
TROUVILLE

GIVERNY
LA ROCHE-GUYON
VÉTHEUIL

BRITANNY

PONT-AVEN
LE POULDU

BELLE-ILE

ILE-DE-FRANCE

PARIS and surrounding region

CHAILLY
BARBIZON SAINT-MAMMÈS

FOREST OF FONTAINEBLEAU
MORET
MARLOTTE

TAHITI

SAINT-RÉMY
ARLES
AIX-EN-PROVENCE
SAINTES-MARIES-DE-LA-MER

MENTON
GRASSE
CAGNES
ANTIBES
L'ESTAQUE

MEDITERRANEAN

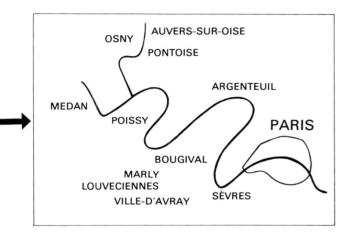

The Impressionist way of feeling was born in the plains of the Ile-de-France and on the Normandy coast, at the time when Cézanne, in his native Provence, felt he must return to a more classical conception of painting. After 1885, Gauguin discovered in Britanny an atmosphere in which his instinct for neo-primitivism could develop.

Van Gogh, who came from Holland, discovered his true self in the sun of Provence; Monet, Renoir and Boudin were attracted by the Southern light and stayed more and more often on the Mediterranean coast.

Donors

Baron R. d'Albenas
Amis du Louvre (Sté des)
Amis du Luxembourg (Sté des)
Mlle d'Angély
M. Bazille
Famille Bazille
E. Béjot
MM. Bernheim-Jeune
M. Mme G. Bernheim de Villers
Héritiers Bernheim de Villers
A. Berthellemy
Fondation Margaret Biddle
M. Mme Blémont
M. Blot
E. Boch
Général Bourjat
Gustave Caillebotte
Famille G. Caillebotte
Comte Isaac de Camondo
Miss M. Cassatt
Mme L. de Chaisemartin
E. Chaplet
Dr et Mme A. Charpentier
Vicomte du Cholet
Georges Clemenceau
C. Comiot
Mme H. Cordier
Alfred Cortot
D. David-Weill
Mme Dortu*
M. Mme J. Doucet
Carle Dreyfus
Mlle Charlotte Dubourg
J.E. Dubrugeaud
Mme H. English
Mme R. Escholier
Fantin-Latour
Mme Fantin-Latour, née Dubourg
Comte, Comtesse de Fels
G. Févre

Dr P. Gachet
Mlle M. Gachet
Paul Gachet
Ph. Gangnat
R. de Gas
Baronne E. Gebhard-Gourgaud
Mme Goekoop de Jong
Baronne R. de Goldschmidt-Rothschild
M. Mme P. Goujon
Katia Granoff
J. Guérard
D. Guérin
Mme Elie Halévy
Mme F.G. Halphen
Mme H.O. Havemeyer
M. Mme N. Hazard
Dr P. Hébert
J. Hill
Mme Howard-Johnston, née Helleu
Mme Huc de Monfreid
Paul Jamot
Mme Jeantaud
Ad. Jullien
Max et Rosy Kaganovitch
A. Kahn
M. Mme R. Kahn-Sriber*
M. Mme R. Koechlin
A. Lacroix
J. Laroche
P. Leclercq
M. Mme C. Lecœur
Mme R. Lecomte
M. Lépine
M. Mme F. Lung
G.B. Lutz
Mr. Mme V. Lyon
C. Mange de Hauke
Mme Marquet*
Dr Martinez
E. May

M. Mme A. Meyer
Mme Vve Michon, née Rimbert
Mme G. Migeon
Eduardo Mollard
M. Monet
Mme J. Monet-Hoschedé
Etienne Moreau-Nélaton
Mme Mottard
Auguste Pellerin
M. Mme J.V. Pellerin
Antonin Personnaz
M. Peytel
M. Philippon
Mme S. Pichon
G. Pimienta
P.E. Pissarro
Princesse Ed. de Polignac, née Singer
Mme Pontillon
John Quinn
J. Reinach
A. Renoir
Les fils de Renoir
T. et G.-H. Rivière
M. Mme E. Rouart
H. Rouart
S. Salz
J. Schmit
E. Senn
Mme G. Signac
P. Soubeiran
M. Mme J. Taillandier
M. Mme Thomas et leurs enfants
Comtesse de Toulouse-Lautrec
Mme Trenel-Pontremoli
G. Viau
Comtesse Vitali
A. Vollard
G. Wildenstein
Mme E. Zola
(avec réserve d'usufruit)

CATALOGUES

Brière : BRIÈRE (G.)
   Musée National du Louvre, catalogue des peintures exposées dans les galeries, I, école française.
   Paris, Editions des Musées Nationaux, 1924.

   Musée National du Louvre, catalogue des peintures et sculptures, exposées au Musée de l'Impressionnisme,
   Paris, Editions des Musées Nationaux, 1947.

Cat. Impr. :
   Musée National du Louvre, catalogue des peintures, pastels, sculptures impressionnistes,
   Paris, Editions des Musées Nationaux, 1958 ; rééd. 1959.

S.A.I. : STERLING (Ch.) et ADHÉMAR (H.)
   Musée National du Louvre, peintures, école française XIXᵉ siècle,
   4 vol., Paris, Editions des Musées Nationaux, 1958-1961.

C.P.t.l. :
   Musée National du Louvre, catalogue des peintures, I, école française,
   Paris, Editions des Musées Nationaux, 1972.

WORKS REFERRED TO IN AN ABBREVIATED FORM

BATAILLE (M.-L.) et WILDENSTEIN (G.), Berthe Morisot, catalogue des peintures, pastels et aquarelles, Paris, 1961.

BENEDITE (L.), Albert Lebourg, Paris, 1923.

BERHAUT (M.), Caillebotte, sa vie et son œuvre, Paris, 1978.

BREESKIN (A.-D.), Mary Cassatt, Washington, 1970.

BOURET (J.), Henri Rousseau, Neuchâtel, 1961.

DAULTE (F.), Alfred Sisley, catalogue raisonné de l'œuvre peint, Lausanne, 1959.

DAULTE (F.), Frédéric Bazille et son temps, Genève, 1952.

DAULTE (F.), Auguste Renoir, catalogue raisonné de l'œuvre peint I, figures (1860-1890), Lausanne, 1971.

DE HAUKE (C.-M.), Seurat et son œuvre, 2 vol. Paris, 1961.

DORRA (H.) et REWALD (J.), Seurat, l'œuvre peint, biographie et catalogue critique, Paris, 1959.

DORTU (M.-G.), Toulouse-Lautrec et son œuvre, 6 vol., Paris, 1971.

FANTIN-LATOUR (Mme), Catalogue de l'œuvre complet (1849-1904) de Fantin-Latour, Paris, 1911.

GRAY (C.), Sculpture and ceramics of Paul Gauguin, Baltimore, 1963.

HEFTING (V.), Jongkind, sa vie, son œuvre, son époque, Paris, 1975.

JAMOT (P.), WILDENSTEIN (G.) et BATAILLE (M.-L.), Manet, 2 vol., Paris, 1932.

LA FAILLE (J.-B. De), L'œuvre de Vincent Van Gogh, catalogue raisonné, 4 vol., Paris-Bruxelles, 1928.

LA FAILLE (J.-B. De), Vincent Van Gogh, Paris, Hypérion, 1939.

LA FAILLE (J.-B. De), The works of Vincent Van Gogh, Amsterdam, 1970.

LEMOISNE (P.-A.), Degas et son œuvre, 4 vol., Paris, 1946-1949.

PISSARRO (L.-R.) et VENTURI (L.), Camille Pissarro, son art, son œuvre, 2 vol., Paris, 1939.

ROBAUT (A.), L'œuvre de Corot, Paris, 1905.

ROBAUT (A.) et CHESNEAU (E.), L'œuvre complète d'Eugène Delacroix, Paris, 1885.

ROUART (D.) et WILDENSTEIN (D.), Edouard Manet, catalogue raisonné, 2 vol., Lausanne-Paris, 1975.

SERRET (G.) et FABIANI (D.), Armand Guillaumin, catalogue raisonné de l'œuvre peint, Paris, 1971.

SCHMIT (R.), Eugène Boudin, 3 vol., Paris, 1973.

TABARANT (A.), Manet et ses œuvres, Paris, 1947.

VALLIER (D.), Tout l'œuvre peint de Henri Rousseau, Paris, 1970.

VENTURI (L.), Cézanne, son art, son œuvre, 2 vol., Paris, 1936.

WILDENSTEIN (G.), Gauguin, Paris, 1964.

WILDENSTEIN (D.), Claude Monet, biographie et catalogue raisonné, I, (1840-1881), Lausanne-Paris, 1974.

Concise catalogue
of works
in the Jeu de Paume Museum

This work revises and completes earlier catalogues to the Museum of Impressionism. We wish to thank the keepers and collaborators who have assisted in the editing of these works; we should also like to thank M. Michel Laclotte, Head Curator of the Department of Paintings; the Head Curator of the Department of Sculpture and Miss Beaulieu, Curator; M. Maurice Sérullaz, Head Curator of the Department of Drawings; the Head Curator of the Department of Art Objects and the Curator of the National Museum of African and Oceanic Arts who placed works from their collections at our disposal.
We have not repeated the titles of Impressionist works included in the Walter-Guillaume and Picasso collections, catalogues of which have already been published.
The Impressionist paintings in the Hélène and Victor Lyon donation exhibited in the Louvre in accordance with the wishes of the donators have been indexed at the end of the catalogue.

WORDS AND ABBREVIATIONS

— acquis en	— acquired in
— ancienne collection	— ex-collection
— attribué au Musée du Louvre	— allotted to the Louvre Museum
par l'Office des Biens privés	by the Private Properties Office
— au crayon	— in pencil
— au revers	— on the back
— B (bois)	— wood
— bois sculpté	— sculpted wood
— cachet	— stamp
— carton	— cardboard
— céramiques	— ceramics
— commande de l'Etat	— commissioned by the State
— craie blanche	— white chalk
— D.h.d. (daté en haut à droite)	— dated top right
— D.b.d. (daté en bas à droite)	— dated bottom right
— dédicacé	— dedicated
— dépôt du Cabinet des Dessins	— on deposit from the Department of drawings
— don, donation	— gift, donation
— en bas	— bottom
— entré en	— received in
— entrelacé	— intertwined
— estampille	— stamp
— étude pour	— study for
— étude inachevée	— uncompleted study
— exécuté en	— executed in
— fusain	— charcoal
— H. hauteur	— height
— inscription b.g. (en bas à gauche)	— inscription bottom left
— L. largeur	— width
— legs, légué	— legacy, bequeathed
— Longueur	— Length
— papier sur toile	— paper on canvas
— pastel et rehauts de gouache sur papier	— pastel touched up with gouache on paper
— peint vers	— painted about
— plâtre	— plaster
— postérieurement	— subsequently
— prêt	— loan
— rehauts de pastel sur esquisse	— touch-ups in pastel on study
au crayon noir sur papier gris	in black pencil on grey paper
— réplique	— replica
— S.b.g. (signé en bas à gauche)	— signed bottom left
— S.b.d. (signé en bas à droite)	— signed bottom right
— S.h.d. (signé en haut à droite)	— signed top right
— S.b. vers la d. (signé en bas vers la droite)	— signed bottom towards right
— S.D.b.d. (signé daté en bas à droite)	— signed dated bottom right
— S.D.b.g. (signé daté en bas à gauche)	— signed dated bottom left
— S.D.b.m. (signé daté au milieu en bas)	— signed dated bottom centre
— S.D.mi.h.g. (signé daté milieu en haut à gauche)	— signed dated top centre left
— sans doute	— probably
— signé	— signed
— sous réserve d'usufruit	— with reservation of usufruct
— terre vernissée	— glazed earthenware
— T. (toile)	— canvas
— verre	— glass
— vitre	— pane

AGUIAR

F.R. 1953-20
HOUSES AT AUVERS
Carton. H. 0.33; W. 0.40.
S.D.b.g.: To my friend Martinez, Aguiar 1875.
Presented by Dr. Martinez, 1953.
Cat. impr. 1 — S.A.I. 2.

F.R. 1953-21
VASE OF FLOWERS
Carton. H. 0.455; L. 0.305.
S.b.g.: Recuerdo de Fontenay. M.A.
Painted ap. 1875.
Presented by Dr. Martinez, 1953.
Cat. impr. 2 — S.A.I. 3.

BAZILLE Frédéric
Montpellier, 1841 - Beaune-la-Rolande (Loiret), 1870.

F.R. 2450
THE PINK DRESS, also known as VIEW OF CASTELNAU
T. H. 1.47; W. 1.10.
S.b.d.: F. Bazille.
Painted in 1864.
(Daulte 9).
Bequest of Marc Bazille, brother of the artist, 1924
(painting reinventoried F.R. 2722, during its transfer
from the Luxembourg to the Louvre in 1929).
Cat. impr. 4 — S.A.I. 40 — C.P.t.l. p. 26.

F.R. 2721
FOREST OF FONTAINEBLEAU
T. H. 0.60; W. 0.73.
Painted in 1865.
(Daulte 11).
Presented by Mme Fantin-Latour, 1905.
Cat. impr. 3 — S.A.I. 41 — C.P.t.l. p. 26.

R.F. 1967-5
THE MAKESHIFT AMBULANCE
(Monet wounded at the Lion d'Or Hotel
at Chailly-en-Bière).
T. H. 0.47; W. 0.65.
Painted in 1865.
(Daulte 14).
Acquired in 1967.
C.P.t.l. p. 26.

F.R. 2749
PORTRAIT OF RENOIR
T. H. 0.62; W. 0.51.
Painted in 1867.
(Daulte 22).
Ex-coll. Claude Renoir.
Lent by the Fine Arts Museum, Algiers.

F.R. 2749
FAMILY REUNION
T. H. 1.52; W. 2.30.
S.D.b.g.: F. Bazille, 1867.
(Daulte 29).
Salon 1868.
Acquired with the participation of Marc Bazille,
brother of the artist, 1905.
Cat. impr. 5 — S.A.I. 42 — C.P.t.l. p. 26.

F.R. 2449
BAZILLE'S STUDIO, rue de la Condamine.

T. H. 0.980; W. 1.285.
S.D.b.d.: F. Bazille, 1870.
(Daulte 48).
Bequeathed by Marc Bazille, brother of the artist,
1924.
Cat. impr. 6 — S.A.I. 43 — C.P.t.l. p. 26.

BERNARD Emile
Lille 1868 - Paris 1941.

INV. 20132
PAUL GACHET (1873-1962)
donator to the National Museums, painter
using the name Louis Van Ryssel
(see under this name).
T. H. 0.40; W. 0.32.
Dedicated in the back: to my friend and companion
Paul Gachet Emile Bernard 1926.
Presented by Paul Gachet to the Modern Art
Museum, 1950; transfered to the Jeu de Paume,
1958.

BONNARD Pierre
Fontenay-aux-Roses 1867 — Le Cannet 1947.

F.R. 1973-9
BLUE NUDE
B. H. 0.30; W. 0.395.
S.b.g.: Bonnard.
Painted ap. 1899-1900.
(H. and J. Dauberville, Bonnard, Catalogue raisonné
de l'œuvre peint, 1888-1905, I, Paris. 1965,
no. 228).
M. and R. Kaganovitch donation, 1973.

F.R. 1973-8
INTERIOR
T. H. 0.53; W. 0.57.
S.b.d.: Bonnard.
Painted ap. 1920.
(H. and J. Dauberville, Bonnard, Catalogue raisonné
de l'œuvre peint, 1920-1930, III, Paris, s.d.,
no. 1028).
M. and R. Kaganovitch donation, 1973.

BOUDIN Eugène
Honfleur (Calvados), 1824 - Deauville (Calvados),
1898.

F.R. 1961-26
THE BEACH AT TROUVILLE, 1864
B. H. 0.26; W. 0.48.
S.D.b.d.: E. Boudin, 1864.
(Schmit 258).
Presented by Eduardo Mollard, 1961.
C.P.t.l. p. 43.

F.R. 3663
THE BEACH AT TROUVILLE, 1865
Carton. H. 0.265; W. 0.405.
S.D.b.d.: E. Boudin, 1865, Trouville (la plage).
(Schmit 351).
Eugène Béjot bequest, 1928, entered in 1932.
Cat. impr. 8 — S.A.I. 121 — C.P.t.l. p. 42.

F.R. 1961-27
THE BEACH AT TROUVILLE, 1867
B. H. 0.32; W. 0.48.
S.D.b.g.: E. Boudin 67. Inscr. b.d. Trouville.

(Schmit 411).
Presented by Eduardo Mollard. 1961.
C.P.t.l. p. 43.

F.R. 1968
BATHERS ON THE BEACH AT TROUVILLE
B. H. 0.31; W. 0.48.
S.D.b.d.: E. Boudin, 1869. inscr. b.g.: Trouville.
(Schmit 494).
Camondo bequest, 1911.
Brière CA. 148 — Cat. impr. 11 — S.A.I. 124.
C.P.t.l. p. 124.

F.R. 1973-10
THE HARBOUR AT ANTWERP
B. H. 0.313; W. 0.467.
S.D.b.g.: E. Boudin 71, Anvers.
(Schmit 646).
M. and R. Kaganovitch donation, 1973.

F.R. 1972-15
THE HARBOUR AT CAMARET
T. H. 0.555; W. 0.895.

F.R. 1972-16
LANDSCAPE WITH WASHERWOMEN
T. H. 0.37; W. 0.58.
S.D.b.d.: E. Boudin 73.
(Schmit 873).
Eduardo Mallard bequest, 1972.

F.R. 1972-17
THE PORT AT BORDEAUX
T. H. 0.41; W. 0.65.
S.D.b.g.: E. Boudin, Bordeaux 74.
(Schmit 976).
Eduardo Mollard bequest, 1972.

F.R. 2716
THE PORT AT BORDEAUX
T. H. 0.705; W. 1.020.
S.D.b.d.: E. Boudin, Bordeaux 74.
(Schmit 966).
Acquired in 1899.
Cat. impr. 14 — S.A.I. 127 — C.P.t.l. p. 43.

M.N.R. 195
SEASCAPE
T. H. 0.85; W. 1.28.
S.D.b.d.: E. Boudin, 1881.
(Schmit 1548).
Attributed to the Louvre Museum by the Private
Property Office, 1950.
C.P.t.l. p. 43.

F.R. 1966
SAILING-BOATS
B. H.: 0.245. W. 0,335.
S.b.g.: E. Boudin. Painted ap. 1885-90.
(Schmit 2002).
Camondo bequest, 1911.
Brière CA. 150 — Cat. impr. 12 — S.A.I. 125 —
C.P.t.l. p. 43.

F.R. 1978-19
THE PORT AT LE HAVRE
(LA BARRE DOCK)
B. H. 0.32; W. 0.41.
S.D.b.g.: Le Havre. E. Boudin 88.
James Hill bequest, 1978.

F.R. 1967
THE JETTY AT DEAUVILLE

B. H. 0.235; W. 0.325.
S.D.b.g. : E. Boudin, 89. Inscr. b.d. Deauville.
(Schmit 2542).
Camondo bequest, 1911.
Brière CA. 149 — Cat. impr. 10 — S.A.I. 123 —
C.P.t.l. p. 43.

F.R. 1972-18
VENICE, LA RIVA DEI SCHIAVONI
T. H. 0.50; W. 0.75.
S.D.b.g : Venice 95. E. Boudin, Venice, June 13.
(Schmit 3395).
Eduardo Mollard bequest, 1972.

CAILLEBOTTE Gustave
Paris, 1848 - Gennevilliers (Hauts-de-Seine), 1894.

F.R. 2718
THE FLOOR-PLANERS
T. H. 1.020; W. 1.465.
S.D.b.d.: G. Caillebotte, 1875.
(Berhaut 28).
Presented by the heirs of Gustave Caillebotte and
of Auguste Renoir, his executor, 1894; entered in
1896.
Cat. impr. 17 — S.A.I. 151 — C.P.t.l. p. 49.

F.R. 2730
ROOFTOPS IN THE SNOW
T. H. 0.64; W. 0.82.
S.b.g.: G. Caillebotte. Painted in 1878.
(Berhaut 107).
Presented by Martial Caillebotte, brother of the
artist, 1894.
Cat. impr. 16 — S.A.I. 152 — C.P.t.l. p. 50.

F.R. 2729
HENRI CORDIER (1849-1929), professor at the
School of Oriental Languages, a friend of the artist.
T. H. 0.64; W. 0.80.
S.D.b.m.: F. Caillebotte, 1883.
(Berhaut 235).
Presented by M. H. Cordier, 1926.
Cat. impr. 18 — S.A.I. 153 — C.P.t.l. p. 50.

F.R. 1954-31
SAILING-BOATS AT ARGENTEUIL
T. H. 0.65; W. 0.55.
S.b.d.: G. Caillebotte, painted ap. 1888.
(Berhaut 359).
Acquired in 1954.
Cat. impr. 19 — S.A.I. 154 — C.P.t.l. p. 50.

F.R. 1971-14
SELF-PORTRAIT
T. H. 0.405; W. 0.325.
S.b.g.: G. Caillebotte. Painted ap. 1889.
(Berhaut 411).
Acquired in 1971.

CALS Adolphe-Félix
Paris, 1810 - Honfleur (Calvados).

F.R. 2840
PORTRAIT OF THE ARTIST
T. H. 0.465; W. 0.387.
S.D.b.g.: Cals, 1851.
Presented by Dr. Georges Vieu, 1930.
Cat. impr. 20 — S.A.I. 155 — C.P.t.l. p. 51.

F.R. 873
STILL-LIFE WITH BACON AND HERRINGS

T. H. 0.34; W. 0.46.
S.D.h.d.: Cals, august 1870.
Presented by M. and Mme Hazard, 1894.
Brière 2933 — Cat. impr. 21 — S.A.I. 156 —
C.P.t.l. p. 51.

F.R. 874
SUNSET OVER HONFLEUR
T. H. 0.34; W. 0.46.
S.D.h.d.: Cals, Honfleur, 1873.
Presentend by M. and Mme Hazard, 1894.
Brière 2934 — Cat. impr. 22 — S.A.I. 157 —
C.P.t.l. p. 51.

M.N.R. 627
FISHERMAN
T. H. 0.25; W. 0.31.
S.D.b.d.: Honfleur 1874 Cals.
Attributed to the Louvre Museum by the Private
Properties Office, 1951.
C.P.t.l. p. 51.

F.R. 1937-19
WOMAN AND CHILD IN AN ORCHARD
T. H. 0.315; W. 0.375.
S.D.b.d.: Cals, Honfleur, 1875.
Antonin Personnaz bequest, 1937.
Cat. impr. 23 — S.A.I. 158 — C.P.t.l. p. 51.

F.R. 1486
LUNCH AT HONFLEUR (CÔTE-DE-GRÂCE)
T. H. 0.455; W. 0.540.
S.D.b.g.: Cals, Honfleur, 1875.
Presented by Henri Rouart, 1903.
Brière 2936 — Cat. impr. 24 — S.A.I. 159 —
C.P.t.l. p. 51.

F.R. 872
WOMEN FRAYING TOW
T. H. 0.51; W. 0.62.
S.D.b.g.: Cals, Honfleur, 1877.
Presented by M. and Mme Hazard, 1894.
Brière 2932 — Cat. impr. 26 — S.A.I. 165 —
C.P.t.l. p. 51.

CASSATT Mary
Alleghenty City (Pennsylvania), 1844 - Château
de Beaufresne at Mesnil-Théribus near Beauvais,
1926.

F.R. 1937-20
WOMAN SEWING
T. H. 0.92; W. 0.63. Painted ap. 1880-82.
S.b.g.: Mary Cassatt.
(Breeskin, 144).
Antonin Personnaz bequest, 1937.
Cat. impr. 27 — S.A.I. 24.

CÉZANNE Paul
Aix-en-Provence, 1839-1906.

M.N.R. 650
HEAD OF AN OLD MAN
(M. Rouvel at Bennecourt?)
T. H. 0.51; W. 0.48 (unifinished painting).
Painted on a canvas representing a procession.
Painted about 1866.
(Venturi 17).
Attributed to the Louvre Museum by the Private
Properties Office, 1951.
Cat. impr. 30 — S.A.I. 247 — C.P.t.l. p. 63.

F.R. 1952-10
MARY-MAGDALENE, also known as SUFFERING
T. H. 1.650; W. 1.255.
Originates from the decor of Le Jas-de-Bouffan, a
property at near Aix-en-Provence belonging to the
artist's family.
Painted ap. 1868-69 (Rewald).
(Venturi 88).
Acquired with a deferred payment from an
anonymous gift from Canada. 1952.
Cat. impr. 29 — S.A.I. 246 — C.P.t.l. p. 62.

F.R. 1963-38
ACHILLE EMPERAIRE (1829-1898), a painter
from Aix.
T. H. 2.00; W. 1.20.
S.b.d. : P. Cézanne.
On top, inscription: Achille Emperaire, painter.
Painted ap. 1868.
(Venturi 88).
Ex-collection Auguste Pellerin.
Anonymous gift, 1964.
C.P.t.l. p. 63.

F.R. 1964-37
STILL-LIFE WITH KETTLE
T. H. 0.645; W. 0.812.
Painted ap. 1869.
(Venturi 70).
Acquired from deferred payment of an anonymous
gift from Canada, with the participation of the heirs
of Gaston Bernheim de Villers and the Society of
Friends of the Louvre, 1963.
C.P.t.l. p. 63.

F.R. 1973-11
THE STRANGLED WOMAN
T. H. 0.31; W. 0.248.
Painted ap. 1870-72.
(Venturi 123).
M. and R. Kaganovitch donation, 1973.

F.R. 1973-12
VILLAGE STREET IN AUVERS
T. H. 0.46; W. 0.553.
S.b.g.: P. Cézanne.
Painted ap. 1872-73.
(Venturi 134).
M. and R. Kaganovitch donation, 1973.

F.R. 1970
THE HOUSE OF THE HANGED MAN, AUVERS-
SUR-OISE
T. H. 0.460; W. 0.66.
S.b.g.: P. Cézanne.
Painted ap. 1873.
(Venturi 133).
Camondo bequest, 1911.
Brière CA 151 — Cat. impr. 38 — S.A.I. 255 —
C.P.t.l. p. 60.

F.R. 1951-31
A MODERN OLYMPIA
T. H. 0.460; W. 0.555.
Painted ap. 1873-74.
(Venturi 225).
Presented by Paul Gachet, 1951.
Cat. impr. 31 — S.A.I. 248 — C.P.t.l. p. 62.

F.R. 1951-32.
DR. GACHET'S HOUSE AT AUVERS
T. H. 0.46; W. 0.38.

Painted ap. 1872.
(Venturi 145).
Presented by Paul Gachet, 1951.
Cat. Impr. 32 — S.A.I. 249 — C.P.t.l. p. 62.

F.R. 1954-5
BOUQUET WITH A YELLOW DAHLIA
T. H. 0.54; W. 0.64.
S.b.d.: P. Cézanne.
Painted ap. 1873.
(Venturi p. 347).
Presented by Paul Gachet, 1954).
Cat. impr. 35 — S.A.I. 252 — C.P.t.l. p. 62.

F.R. 1954-6
GREEN APPLES
T. H. 0.26; W. 0.32.
Painted ap. 1873.
(Venturi 66).
Presented by Paul Gachet, 1954.
Cat. impr. 33 — S.A.I. 250 — C.P.t.l. p. 62.

F.R. 1954-7
THE ARTIST'S ACCESSORIES. STILL-LIFE WITH
MEDALLION OF PHILIPPE SOLARI
T. H. 0.60; W. 0.80.
Painted ap. 1873.
(Venturi 67).
Presented by Paul Gachet, 1954.
Cat. impr. 36 — S.A.I. 253 — C.P.t.l. p. 62.

F.R. 1954-8
CROSSING AT THE RUE RÉMY AT AUVERS
T. H. 0.380; W. 0.455.
Painted ap. 1873.
Presented by Paul Gachet, 1954.
Cat. impr. 37 — S.A.I. 254 — C.P.t.l. p. 62.

F.R. 1971
DAHLIAS
T.H. 0.73; W. 0.54.
Painted at Auvers ap. 1873.
(Venturi 179).
Camondo bequest, 1911.
Brière CA. 152 — Cat. impr. 39 — S.A.I. 256 —
C.P.t.l. p. 61.

F.R. 1951-33
FLOWERS IN A DELFT VASE
T. H. 0.41; W. 0.27.
S.b.g. : P. Cézanne.
Painted ap. 1873.
(Venturi 183).
Presented by Paul Gachet, 1951.
Cat. impr. 34 — S.A.I. 251 — C.P.t.l. p. 62.

F.R. 1947-29
SELF-PORTRAIT
T. H. 0.64; W. 0.53.
Painted ap. 1873-76.
(Venturi 288).
Presented by J. Laroche, 1947, with condition of
usufruct in favour of his son, who handed it over
to the Museum in 1969.
C.P.t.l. p. 61.

F.R. 1955-20
THE BRIDGE AT MAINCY, near Melun.
T. H. 0.585; W. 0.725.
Painted in 1879-80 (Rewald).
(Venturi 396).
Acquired from deferred payment of an anonymous

gift from Canada, 1955.
Cat. imp. 43 — S.A.I. 260 — C.P.t.l. p. 61.

F.R. 2760
FARM-YARD AT AUVERS
T. H. 0.65; W. 0.54.
Painted ap. 1879-80.
(Venturi 326).
Gustave Caillebotte bequest, 1894. Entered 1896.
Cat. impr. 40 — S.A.I. 257 — C.P.t.l. p. 61.

F.R. 2324
POPLARS
T. H. 0.65; W. 0.81.
Painted ap. 1879-82.
(Venturi 335).
Joseph Reinach bequest, 1921.
Cat. impr. 41 — S.A.I. 258 — C.P.t.l. p. 63.

M.N.R. 228
SELF-PORTRAIT
T. H. 0.225; W. 0.145.
Painted ap. 1877-80.
(Venturi 371).
Attributed to the Louvre Museum by the Private
Properties Office, 1950.
Cat. impr. 42 — S.A.I. 259 — C.P.t.l. p. 63.

F.R. 2761
L'ESTAQUE. View over the bay of Marseilles.
T. H. 0.595; W. 0.730.
S.b.d. : P. Cézanne (practically obliterated).
Painted ap. 1878-79.
(Venturi 428).
Gustave Caillebotte bequest, 1894; entered in
1896.
Cat. impr. 44 — S.A.I. 261 — C.P.t.l. p. 61.

F.R. 2818
STILL-LIFE WITH SOUP-TUREEN
T. H. 0.650; W. 0.815.
Painted ap. 1877.
(Venturi 494).
Auguste Pellerin bequest, 1929.
Cat. impr. 45 — S.A.I. 262 — C.P.t.l. p. 61.

F.R. 1973
THE BLUE VASE
T. H. 0.61; W. 0.50.
Painted ap. 1885-87.
(Venturi 512).
Camondo bequest, 1911.
Brière CA 154 — Cat. impr. 47 — S.A.I. 264 —
C.P.t.l. p. 61.

F.R. 2819
STILL-LIFE WITH BASKET
T. H. 0.65; W. 0.81.
S.b.d. : P. Cézanne.
Auguste Pellerin bequest, 1929.
Cat. impr. 49 — S.A.I. 266 — C.P.t.l. p. 6.

F.R. 1973-55
FISHING-BOAT
T. H. 0.325; W. 0.295
Central fragment of a dessus-de-porte executed for
V. Choquet ap. 1890, later cup up into three
pieces; the lateral parts are in the Walter Guillaume
collection (F.R. 1960-12 and F.R. 1960-13).
It has been possible to reconstitute this work in
its original state; it will be presented with the
Walter Guillaume collection.

(Venturi 583).
Acquired in 1973.

F.R. 1965-3
BATHERS
T. H. 0.60; W. 0.82.
Painted ap. 1890-92.
(Venturi 580).
Presented by baroness Eva Gebhard-Gourgaud,
1965.
C.P.t.l. p. 63.

F.R. 1969
THE CARD-PLAYERS
T. H. 0.475; W. 0.570.
Painted ap. 1890-95.
(Venturi 558).
Camondo bequest 1911.
Brière CA. 153 — Cat. impr. 48 — S.A.I. 265 —
C.P.t.l. p. 265.

F.R. 1956-13
WOMAN WITH COFFEE-POT
T. H. 1.305; W. 965.
Painted ap. 1890-95.
(Venturi 574).
Presented by M. and Mme Jean-Victor Pellerin,
1956.
Cat. impr. 50 — S.A.I. 267 — C.P.t.l. p. 63.

F.R. 1949-30
BATHERS
T. H. 0.220; W. 0.325.
Painted ap. 1890-1900.
(Venturi 585).
Acquired in 1849.
Cat. impr. 46 — S.A.I. 263 — C.P.t.l. p. 62.

F.R. 2807
STILL-LIFE WITH ONIONS
T. H. 0.66; W. 0.82.
Painted ap. 1895.
(Venturi 730).
Auguste Pellerin bequest, 1929.
Cat. impr. 51 — S.A.I. 268 — C.P.t.l. p. 61.

F.R. 1972
APPLES AND ORANGES
T. H. 0.74; W. 0.93.
Painted ap. 1895-1900.
(Venturi 732).
Camonde bequest, 1911.
Brière CA. 155 — Cat. impr. 52 — S.A.I. 269 —
C.P.t.l. p. 61.

COROT Jean-Baptiste-Camille
Paris, 1796-1875.

R.F. 1612
FISHERMENS' HOUSES AT SAINTE-ADRESSE
T. H. 0.28; W. 0.42.
S.b.g. : Corot; painted ap. 1830.
(Robaut 239).
Etienne Moreau-Nélaton donation, 1906.
Brière M. 16 — S.A.I. 371 — C.P.t.l. p. 88.

F.R. 1973-13
STRANDED SAILING-BOATS AT TROUVILLE
T. H. 0.21; W. 0.235.
S.b.g. : Corot.
Painted ap. 1830.

(Robaut, 231).
M. and R. Kaganovitch donation, 1973.

F.R. 1620
LA ROCHELLE
T. H. 0.27; W. 0.42. 1851.
(Robaut 671).
Etienne Moreau-Nélaton donation, 1906.
Brière M. 28 — S.A.I. 396 — C.P.t.l. p. 89.

F.R. 1961-23
TOWER AT THE WATER'S EDGE
T. H. 0.30; W. 0.235.
S.b.g.: Corot, painted ap. 1855-65.
(Robaut 1447).
Eduardo Mollard donation, 1961.
C.P.t.l. p. 100.

F.R. 1352
THE ROAD TO SÈVRES
T. H. 0.34; W. 0.39.
S.b.d.: Corot; painted ap. 1855-65.
(Robaut 1464).
Thomy-Thiéry bequest, 1902.
Brière T. 2803 — S.A.I. 421 — C.P.t.l. p. 87.

COURBET Gustave
Ornans (Doubs), 1817 - La Tour-de-Pelz, near
Vevey (Switzerland), 1877.

F.R. 1973-14
CHERRY-TREE BLOSSOM
T. H. 0.32; W. 0.405.
S.D.b.g.: 71 G. Courbet; à d. Ste Pélagie.
M. and R. Kaganovitch donation, 1973.

DAUBIGNY Charles-François
Paris 1817-1878.

F.R. 1362
CANAL-BOATS
B. H. 0.38; W. 0.67.
S.D.b.d.: Daubigny 1865.
Thomy-Thiéry bequest, 1902.
Brière T. 2820 — S.A.I. 512 — C.P.t.l. p. 111.

DAUMIER Honoré
Marseille, 1808 - Valmondois (Val-d'Oise), 1879.

F.R. 1973-15
THE KISS
B. H. 0.237; W. 0.298.
Monogr. b.g.: H.D.
Painted ap. 1845.
(K.E. Maison, Daumier, London 1968, 0,6).
M. and R. Kaganovitch donation, 1973.

DEGAS Hilaire-Germain-Edgar de Gas, known as Degas
Paris 1834-1917.

F.R. 2649
SELF-PORTRAIT
T. H. 0.810; W. 0.645.
(Lemoisne 5).
Acquired in 1927 at the René de Gas sale.
Cat. impr. 53 — S.A.I. 601 — C.P.t.l. p. 125.

F.R. 3663
GIOVANNA BELLELLI (born 1848), known
as "Nini", the artist's cousin, later Marquise
Ferdinando Lignola.
T. H. 0.26; W. 0.23.
On the back of the canvas, an inscription in Degas
handwriting: Nini Bellelli. Ap. 1856, Naples.
Degas.
Presented by the Society of Friends of the Louvre,
1932.
Cat. impr. 54 — S.A.I. 602. — C.P.t.l. p. 126.

F.R. 3661
HILAIRE-RENÉ DE GAS (1770-1858)
The artist's grandfather at the age of 87, migrated
to Naples, where he became a banker.
T. H. 0.53; W. 0.41.
D.h.d.: Capdimonte, 1857.
(Lemoigne 27).
Presented by the Society of Friends of the Louvre,
1932.
Cat. impr. 55 — S.A.I. 603. — C.P.t.l. p. 126.

F.R. 3584
MARGUERITE DE GAS (1842-1895)
The artist's sister, later Mme Henri Fèvre.
T. H. 0.27; W. 0.22.
Painted ap. 1858-60.
(Lemoisne 61).
Acquired in 1931
Cat. impr. 57 — S.A.I. 605 — C.p.t.l. p. 126.

F.R. 3585
MARGUERITE DE GAS (1842-1,895)
Sister of the artist
T. H. 0.80; W. 0.54.
Painted ap. 1858-60.
(Lemoisne 60).
Acquired in 1931).
Cat. impr. 56 — S.A.I. 604 — C.P.t.l. p. 126.

F.R. 2210
THE BELLELLI FAMILY, Baron Gennaro Bellelli
(1812-1864), senator of the kingdom of Italy;
his wife, born Clothilde-Laure de Gas, known as
"Laurette", the artist's aunt; their daughters,
Giovanna (born 1848) and Guilia (1851-1922).
T. H. 2.00; W. 2.50.
(Lemoisne 79).
Acquired in 1918 with the help of Compte and
Comtesse de Fels, and thanks to René de Gas.
Cat. impr. 59 — S.A.I. 607 — C.P.t.l. p. 124.

F.R. 226
STUDY OF HANDS
T. H. 0.38. W. 0.46
S.h.d.: Degas.
Study of the hands of Baroness Bellelli.
(F. R. 2210).
(Lemoisne 181, with date 1868).
Presented by the Society of Friends of the
Luxembourg, 1919.
Cat. impr. 65 — S.A.I. 608 — C.P.t.l. p. 125.

F.R. 36085
SEMIRAMIS FOUNDING BABYLONE
Pastel H. 0.40; W. 0.67.
Study for F. R. 2207.
(Lemoisne 85).
Presented by M. Edouard Senn, 1976.
On deposit from the Department of Drawings.

F.R. 2207
SEMIRAMIS FOUNDING BABYLONE
T. H. 1.51; W. 2.58.
S.b.d.: Degas.
Painted in 1861.
(Lemoisne 12).
Acquired in 1918.
Cat. impr. 58 — S.A.I. 606 — C.P.t.l. p. 124.

F.R. 1982
GENTLEMAN-RIDERS' RACE BEFORE THE START
T. H. 0.485; W. 0.615
S.D.b.d.: Degas, 1862.
Partially repainted by the artist
(Lemoisne 101)
Camondo bequest, 1911.
Brière CA. 158 — Cat. impr. 60 — S.A.I. 609.
C.P.t.l. p. 124.

F.R. 2650
THÉRÈSE DE GAS (†1897),
sister of the artist, later Mme Edmond Morbilli.
T. H. 0.89; W. 0.67.
Painted ap. 1863, the year of her marriage.
(Lemoisne 109).
Acquired in 1927.
Cat. impr. 61 — S.A.I. 610 — C.P.t.l. p. 125.

F.R. 3586
DEGAS AND EVARISTE DE VALERNES
(1817-1896), painter and friend of the artist.
T. H. 1.16; W. 0.89.
Painted ap. 1864.
(Lemoisne 116).
Presented by Gabriel Fèvre, the artist's nephew,
1931.
Cat. impr. 62 — S.A.I. 611 — C.P.t.l. p. 126

F.R. 2208
BATTLE-SCENE DURING THE MIDDLE AGES or
THE MISFORTUNES OF NEW ORLEANS, formerly
known as the Misfortunes of the City of Orleans.
Paper on T. H. 0.85; W. 1.47.
S.b.d.: Ed. De Gas.
1865 Salon.
(Lemoisne 124).
Acquired in 1918.
Cat. impr. 63 — S.A.I. 612 — C.p.t.l. p. 124.

F.R. 2430
PORTRAIT OF A YOUNG WOMAN
T. H. 0.27; W. 0.22.
S.h.d.: Degas.
Painted in 1867.
(Lemoisne 163).
Acquired in 1924.
Cat. impr. 64 — S.A.I. 613 — C.P.t.l. p. 125.

M.N.R. 217
EVARISTE DE VALERNES (1817-96), painter,
childhood friend of the artist.
T. H. 0.59; W. 0.46.
S.d.b.d.: Degas 1868.
(Lemoisne 177).
Attributed to the Louvre Museum by the Private
Properties Office, 1950.
Cat. impr. 66 — S.A.I. 614 — C.P.t.l. p. 127.

F.R. 2582
THE VIOLINCELLIST PILLET,
of the Opera-House orchestra.
T. H. 0.505; W. 0.610.

Painted ap. 1868-69.
(Lemoisne 188).
Presented by Charles Comiot through the interme-
diary of the Society of Friends of the Louvre, 1926.
Cat. impr. 67 — S.A.I. 615 — C.P.t.l. p. 125.

F.R. 2417
THE ORCHESTRA OF THE OPERA-HOUSE
In the foreground, Désiré Dihau (1833-1909),
bassoonist in the Opera-House Orchestra, friend
of Degas.
T. H. : 0.565; W. 0.462.
S.b.d. on the chair: Degas.
Painted ap. 1868-69
(Lemoisne 186).
Acquired by Mlle Marie Dihau, sister of Désiré
with reservation of usufruct, 1924; entered the
Louvre Museum in 1935.
Cat. impr. 68 — S.A.I. 616 — C.P.t.l. p. 125.

F.R. 3736
PAGANS, Spanish singer, with
AUGUSTE DE GAS (1807-1874), the artist's father.
T. H. 0.545; W. 0.400.
Painted ap. 1869.
(Lemoisne 256).
Another version at the Museum of Fine Arts,
Boston.
Presented by the Society of Friends of the Louvre,
1933, with the participation of D. David-Weill.
Cat. impr. 69 — S.A.I. 617 — C.P.t.l. p. 126.

F.R. 2416
MADEMOISELLE DIHAU AT THE PIANO
Marie Dihau (1843-1935), painist at the Colonna
concerts.
T. H. 0.450; W. 0.325.
Painted ap. 1869-72.
(Lemoisne 263).
Acquired by Mlle Marie Dihau, with reservation
of usufruct, 1924; entered the Louvre Museum,
1935.
Cat. impr. 73 — S.A.I. 621 — C.P.t.l. p. 125.

F.R. 28829
THE IRONING-WOMAN
Charcoal, white chalk and pastel.
H. 0.74; W. 0.61.
S.b.d.: Degas.
Executed in 1869.
Personal bequest, entered in 1937 with no. F. R.
1937-25.
On deposit from the Department of Drawings.
Cat. impr. 70 — S.A.I. 618.

F.R. 31199
CLIFFS BY THE SEA
Pastel. H. 0.324; W. 0.469.
Red stamp from the Degas sale.
Executed in 1869.
(Lemoisne 199).
Presented by Baronness Eva Gebhard-Gourgaud,
1965.
On deposit from the Department of Drawings.

F.R. 31200
STUDY OF SKY
Pastel. H. 0.290; W. 0.480.
Red stamp of the Degas sale.
(Lemoisne 219).
Presented by Baroness Eva Gebhard-Gourgaud,
1965.
On deposit from the Department of Drawings.

F.R. 31203
TREES BORDERING A PLAIN
Pastel. H. 0.315; W. 0.485.
Red stamp of the Degas sale.
(Lemoisne 284).
Presented by Baroness Eva Gebhard-Gourgaud,
1965.
Depository of the Department of Drawings.

F.R. 2825
JEANTAUD, LINET AND LAINÉ, friends of the artist.
T. H. 0.38; W. 0.46.
S.D.h.g.: Degas, March 1871.
(Lemoisne 287).
Presented by Mme Jeantaud, 1929.
Cat. impr. 74 — S.A.I. 622 — C.P.t.l. p. 126.

F.R. 1986
WOMAN WITH A VASE
T. H. 0.66; W. 0.54.
S.D.b.g. (twice): Degas, 1872.
(Lemoisne 305).
Camondo bequest, 1911.
Brière CA. 159 — Cat. impr. 76 — S.A.I. 624 —
C.P.t.l. p. 124.

F.R. 1986
THE CHIROPODIST
Paper on T. H. 0.61; W. 0.46.
S.D.b.g.: Degas, 1873.
(Lemoisne 323).
Camondo bequest, 1911.
Brière CA. 161 — Cat. impr. 78 — S.A.I. 625 —
C.P.t.l. p. 123.

R.F. 1977
THE GREEN-ROOM OF THE OPERA-HOUSE
IN THE RUE LE PELETIER
T. H. 0.32; W. 0.46
S.b.d.: Degas.
Painted 1872
(Lemoisne 298).
Camondo bequest, 1911.
Brière CA. 160 — Cat. impr. 77 — S.A.I. 625 —
C.P.t.l. p. 123

F.R. 1978
STAGE-REHEARSAL OF A BALLET
T. H. 0.65; W. 0.81.
S.b.d.: Degas
Painted 1874.
(Lemoisne 340).
Camondo bequest, 1911.
Brière CA. 182 — Cat. impr. 79 — S.A.I. 627 —
C.P.t.l. p. 123.

F.R. 1976
THE DANCING-CLASS
T. H. 0.85; W. 0.75.
Painted ap. 1874.
(Lemoisne 341).
Camondo bequest, 1911.
Brière CA. 163 — Cat. impr. 80 — S.A.I. 628 —
C.P.t.l. p. 123.

F.R. 1970-38
MADAME JEANTAUD AT HER MIRROR
T. H. 0.70; W. 0.84.
S.b.d.: Degas.
Painted ap. 1875.
Originally from the J. Doucet collection.
Bequest from Jean-Edouard Dubrujaud, with

reservation of usufruct in favour of his son, Jean
Angladon-Dubruhaud, 1970.
Usufruct abandonned in 1970.
C.P.t.l. p. 127.

F.R. 1984
AT THE CAFÉ, also known as ABSINTHE
T. H. 0.92; W. 0.68.
S.b. to the left: Degas.
Painted in 1876.
(Lemoisne 393).
Camondo bequest, 1911.
Brière CA. 164 — Cat. impr. 81 — S.A.I. 629 —
C.P.t.l. p. 124.

F.R. 4040
END OF AN ARABESQUE
Mixed media: oil and pastel.
T. H. 0.674; W. 0.38.
S.b.g.: Degas.
Executed ap. 1877.
(Lemoisne 418).
Camondo bequest, 1911.
On deposit from the Department of Drawings.
Cat. impr. 83 — S.A.I. 631.

F.R. 4039
DANCER WITH BOUQUET, CURTSEYING
Pastel on paper pasted on canvas.
H. 0.72; W. 0.775.
S.h.g.: Degas.
Executed ap. 1877.
(Lemoisne 474).
Camondo bequest, 1911.
On deposit from the Department of Drawings.
Cat. impr. 87 — S.A.I. 635.

F.R. 12258
THE STAR, also known as DANCER ON THE
STAGE
Pastel. H. 0.60; W. 0.44.
S.h.g.: Degas.
Executed ap. 1878.
(Lemoisne 491).
Caillebotte bequest, 1894; entered in 1896.
On deposit from the Department of Drawings
Cat. impr. 88 — S.A.I. 636.

F.R. 2444
AT THE STOCK-EXCHANGE
T. H. 1.00; W. 0.82.
Painted ap. 1878-79.
(Lemoisne 499).
Presented by Ernest May, with reservation
of usufruct, 1923; entered 1926.
Cat. impr. 89 — S.A.I. 637 — C.P.t.l. p. 125.

F.R. 1981
RACE-HORSES IN FRONT OF THE STANDS
T. H. 0.46; W. 0.41.
S.b.g. : Degas.
Painted ap. 1879.
(Lemoisne 262).
Camondo bequest, 1911.
Brière CA. 165 — Cat. impr. 72 — S.A.I. 620 —
C.P.t.l. p. 124.

F.R. 1980
THE RACE-COURSE
RIDERS BESIDE A CARRIAGE
T. H. 0.66; W. 0.81.
S.d.: Degas.

Painted ap. 1877-80.
(Lemoisne 461).
Camondo bequest, 1911.
Brière CA. 166 — Cat. impr. 86 — S.A.I. 634 —
C.P.t.l. p. 123.

F.R. ·12260
A SINGER
Pastel touched up with gouache on pale grey paper.
H. 0.618; W. 0.475.
S.b.g. in pencil: Degas.
Executed ap. 1880.
(Lemoisne 605).
Caillebotte bequest, 1894; entered 1896
On deposit from the Department of Drawings.
Cat. impr. 103 — S.A.I. 639.

F.R. 4037
THREE STUDIES OF THE HEAD OF THE DANCER
Pastel on buff-coloured paper.
H. 0.180; W. 0.568.
S.b.d.: Degas.
Ap. 1880.
(Lemoisne 593).
Camondo bequest 1911.
On deposit from the Department of Drawings.

F.R. 4043
WOMAN IN HER BATH, SPONGING HER LEG
Pastel. H. 0.917; W. 0.41.
S.b.g.: Degas.
Executed ap. 1883.
(Lemoisne 728).
On deposit from the Department of Drawings.
Cat. impr. 92 — S.A.I. 641.

F.R. 1985
IRONING-WOMEN
T. H. 0.750; W. 0.815.
S.h.d.: Degas.
Painted ap. 1884.
(Lemoisne 785).
Camondo bequest, 1911.
Brière CA. 168 — Cat. impr. 93 — S.A.I. 642 —
C.P.t.l. p. 124.

F.R. 4045
AFTER THE BATH, WOMAN DRYING HER FEET
Pastel on cardboard. H. 0.543; W. 0.524.
S.b.d.: Degas.
Executed in 1886.
(Lemoisne 874).
Camondo bequest, 1911.
On deposit from the Department of Drawings.
Cat. impr. 96 — S.A.I. 644.

F.R. 4046
THE TUB
Pastel on cardboard. H. 0.60; W. 0.83.
S.D.h.d.: Degas, 86.
(Lemoisne 872).
Camondo bequest, 1911.
On deposit from the Department of Drawings.
Cat. impr. 95 — S.A.I. 645.

F.R. 1979
DANCERS MOUNTING THE STAIRS
T. H. 0.390; W. 0.895.
S.b.g.: Degas.
Painted ap. 1886-90.
(Lemoisne 894).
Camondo bequest, 1911.

Brière CA. 167 — Cat. impr. 97 — S.A.I. 646 —
C.P.t.l. p. 123.

F.R. 1951-10
DANCERS IN BLUE
T. H. 0.850; W. 0.755.
S.b.g.: Degas.
Painted ap. 1890.
(Lemoisne 1014).
Another version in the Metropolitan Museum,
New York.
Presented by Dr. and Mme Albert Charpentier,
1951.
Cat. impr. 99 — S.A.I. 648 — C.P.t.l. p. 126.

F.R. 1961-28.
HARLEQUIN AND COLOMBINE
B. H. 0.330; W. 0.235.
Stamped bottom right in red: Degas.
Painted ap. 1886-90.
(Lemoisne 1111).
Presented by Eduardo Mollard, 1961.
C.P.t.l. p. 126.

F.R. 4042
WOMAN WASHING IN HER TUB
Coloured pencils and pastel on cardboard.
H. 0.318; W. 0.474.
S.b.g.: Degas.
Executed ap. 1892.
(Lemoisne 1121).
Camondo bequest, 1911.
On deposit from the Department of Drawings.
Cat. impr. 101 — S.A.I. 649.

F.R. 2137
TALL DANCER, CLOTHED
Bronze. H. 0.98.
Entered on the Louvre Museum in 1930; on deposit
from the Department of Sculptures.
Cat. 1922-1933, no. 1790 — Cat. impr. 448.

DELACROIX Eugène
Charenton-Saint-Maurice (Val-de-Marne), 1796 -
Paris, 1863.

F.R. 31719
BUNCH OF FLOWERS
Water-colour, gouache, touched up with pastel over
a drawing in black pencil on grey paper.
H. 0.650; W. 0.654.
(Robert-Chesneau 1042).
César Mange de Hauke bequest, 1965.
On deposit from the Department of Drawing.
This work was copied by Cézanne.
(Moscow, Pouchkine Museum).

DERAIN André
Chatou, 1880 - Garches, 1954.

F.R. 1973-16
WESTMINSTER BRIDGE
T. H. 0.81; W. 1.00.
S.b.d.: Derain.
Painted ap. 1906.
M. and R. Kaganovitch donation, 1973.

F.R. 1977-4
CHILD RUNNING ON THE BEACH
T. H. 0.244; W. 0.193.

S.b.g.: a. derain.
M. and R. Kaganovitch Donation.

DIAZ DE LA PEÑA Narcisse
Bordeaux, 1807 - Menton (Alpes-Maritimes), 1876.

F.R. 1972-19
LANDSCAPE
T. H. 0.322; W. 0.435.
Stamped bottom right in red capital letters:
N. DIAZ.
Eduardo Mollard bequest, 1972.

DUBOURG Victoria
(Mme Fantin-Latour).
Paris, 1840 - Buré (Orne), 1926.

F.R. 3766
CORNER OF A TABLE, still-life.
T. H. 0.52; W. 0.63.
S.h.g.: V. Dubourg.
1901 Salon.
Originally from the Luxembourg Museum.
S.A.I. 793 — C.P.t.l. p. 148.

INV. 20054
FLOWERS IN A VASE
T. H. 0.425; W. 0.367.
S.D.b.g.: V. Dubourg, 1910.
Originally in the Luxembourg Museum.
A.S.I. 793 - C.P.t.l. p. 148.

FANTIN-LATOUR Henri
Grenoble, 1836 - Buré (Orne), 1904.

WOMAN READING, Marie Fantin-Latour, sister
of the artist.
T. H. 1.00; W. 0.83.
S.D.h.g.: Fantin, 1861.
1861 Salon.
(Fantin-Latour 169).
M. and Mme Raymond Koechin bequest, 1931.
Cat. impr. 104 — S.A.I. 827 — C.P.t.l. p. 159.

F.R. 1666
NARCISSI AND TULIPS
T. H. 0.460; W. 0.386.
S.h.g.: Fantin D.h.g. 1862
(Fantin-Latour 195).
Etienne Moreau-Nélaton donation, 1906
Brière M. 65 — Cat. impr. 105 — S.A.I. 828 —
C.P.t.l. p. 158.

F.R. 1664
HOMMAGE TO DELACROIX
From left to right: Cordier, Duranty, Legros,
Fantin-Latour, Whistler, Champfleury, Manet,
Bracquemond, Baudelaire, de Balleroy.
T. H. 1.60; W. 2.50.
S.D.h.g.: Fantin, 1864.
1864 Salon.
(Fantin-Latour 227).
Etienne Moreau-Nélaton Donation, 1906.
Brière M. 66 — Cat. impr. 106 — S.A.I. 829 —
C.P.t.l. p. 157.

M.N.R. 227
FLOWERS AND FRUIT
T. H. 0.64; W. 0.57.
S.D.h.d.: Fantin, 1865.

(Fantin-Latour 276 bis).
Attributed to the Louvre Museum by the Private
Properties Office, 1950.
Cat. impr. 107 — S.A.I. 830 — C.P.t.l. p. 159.

F.R. 1974-17
ANTOINE VOLLON (1833-1900).
T. H. 0.302; W. 0.18.
S.D.h.d.: Fantin 1865.
(Fantin-Latour 273).
Fragment of a large composition entitled "The
Toast", exhibited at the 1865 *Salon*, and later
destroyed by the artist who kept only three frag-
ments, including this portrait of the painter Vollon.
Acquired in 1974.

R.F. 3637
THE STUDIO IN THE RUE DES BATIGNOLLES
T. H. 0.29; W. 0.39.
S.b.g.: Fantin.
Painted ap. 1870.
Study for F.R. 729.
(Fantin-Latour 210).
Presented by the artist, 1899.
Cat. impr. 108 — S.A.I. 831 — C.P.t.l. p. 159.

F.R. 729
THE STUDIO IN THE RUE DES BATIGNOLLES
From left to right: Otto Schölderer, Manet, Renoir,
Zacharie, Astruc, Emile Zola, Edmond Maître,
Bazille, Monet.
T. H.: 2.040; W. 2.735.
S.D.b.g.: Fantin, 70.
1870 *Salon*.
(Fantin-Latour 409).
Acquired 1892.
Cat. impr. 109 — S.A.I. 832 — C.P.t.l. p. 157.

F.R. 159
A CORNER OF THE TABLE
From left to right: Paul Verlaine, Arthur Rimbaud,
Elzéar Bonnier, Léon Valade, Emile Blémont,
Jean Aicard, Ernest d'Hervilly, Camille Pelletan.
T. H. 1.60; W. 2.25.
S.D.h.d.: Fantin, 1872.
1872 *Salon*.
(Fantin-Latour 577).
Presented by Léon-Emile Petitdidier, also known
as Emile Blémont, and Mme Blémont, with
reservation of usufruct, 1910; usufruct abandoned,
1920.
Brière 3078 — Cat. impr. 110 — S.A.I. 833 —
C.P.t.l. p. 158.

R.F. 1665
STUDY OF A FEMALE NUDE
T. H. 0.445; W. 2.70.
S.D.b.d.: Fantin, 1872.
(Fantin-Latour 580).
Moreau-Nélaton donation, 1906.
Brière M. 67 — Cat. impr. 117 — S.A.I. 834 —
C.P.t.l. p. 157.

F.R. 3629
VICTORIA DUBOURG (1840-1926), painter, later
the artist's wife.
T. H. 0.925; W. 0.760.
S.D.h.g.: Fantin, 73.
1873 *Salon*.
(Fantin-Latour 647).
Presented by the artist in 1902.
Cat. impr. 111 — S.A.I. 835 — C.P.t.l. p. 158.

F.R. 2349
THE DUBOURG FAMILY
M. and Mme Dubourg and their daughters,
Victoria, the artist's wife, and Charlotte.
T. H. 1.465; W. 1.705.
S.D.b.g.: Fantin, 78.
1878 *Salon*
(Fantin-Latour 867).
Presented by Mme Fantin-Latour, the artist's wife,
with reservation of usufruct, 1921; entered in
1926.
Cat. impr. 113 — S.A.I. 837 — C.P.t.l. p. 158.

F.R. 2348
CHARLOTTE DUBOURG (1850-1921), sister
of the artist's wife.
T. H. 1.180; W. 0.925.
S.D.h.g.: Fantin, 82.
1887 *Salon*
(Fantin-Latour 1058).
Bequeathed by Charlotte Dubourg, 1921.
Cat. impr. 114 — S.A.I. 838 — C.P.t.l. p. 158.

F.R. 1961-25
ROSES IN A GLASS BOWL
T. H. 0.365; W. 0.460.
S.D.h.d.: Fantin, 82.
Presented by Eduardo Mollard, 1961.
C.P.t.l. p. 159.

F.R. 2173
AROUND THE PIANO
From left to right: Adolphe Jullien, Boisseau,
Chabrier, Camille Benoît, Edmond Maître, Lascaux,
Vincent d'Indy, Amédée Pigeon.
T. H. 1.60; W. 2.22.
S.D.h.d.: Fantin, 85.
1885 *Salon*.
(Fantin-Latour 1194).
Presented by Adolphe Jullien, with reservation
of usufruct, 1915. Usufruct abandonned, 1919.
Cat. impr. 115 — S.A.I. 839 — C.P.t.l. p. 158.

F.R. 2174
ADOLPHE JULLIEN (1840-1932),
historian and musical critic, friend and
historiographer of the artist.
T. H. 1.60; W. 1.50.
S.D.b.g.: Fantin, 87.
1887 *Salon*.
(Fantin-Latour 1292).
Presented by Adolphe Jullien with reservation
of usufruct, 1915; usufruct abandonned, 1919.
Cat. impr. 116 — S.A.I. 840 — C.P.t.l. p. 158.

F.R. 1086
NIGHT
T. H. 0.61; W. 0.75.
S.b.g.: Fantin.
Painted in 1897.
(Fantin-Latour 1652).
Acquired at the 1897 *Salon*.
Cat. impr. 119 — S.A.I. 842 — C.P.t.l. p. 157.

F.R. 1937-62
BEDTIME
T. H. 0.295; W. 0.220.
S.b.g.: Fantin.
Grisaille (Fantin-Latour 2248).
Antonin Personnaz bequest, 1937.
Cat. impr. 118 — S.A.I. 841 — C.P.t.l. p. 159.

GAUGUIN Paul
Paris, 1848 - Atouana (Domenica), 1903.

F.R. 1941-27
THE SEINE AT THE IÉNA BRIDGE UNDER SNOW
T. H. 0.650; W. 0.925.
S.D.b.d.: P. Gauguin, 1875.
(Wildenstein 13).
Bequeathed by Payl Jamot, 1941.
Cat. impr. 129 — S.A.I. 897 — C.P.t.l. p. 172.

M.N.R. 219
STILL-LIFE WITH MANDOLIN
T. H. 0.61; W. 0.51.
S.D.b.d.: P. Gauguin, 85.
(Wildenstein 173).
Attributed to the Louvre Museum by the Private
Properties Office, 1950.
Cat. impr. 129 — S.A.I. 898 — C.P.t.l. p. 174.

F.R. 1965-17
WASHERWOMEN AT PONT-AVEN
T. H. 0.71; W. 0.90.
S.D.b.g.: P. Gauguin, 86.
(Wildenstein 196).
Acquired in 1965.
C.P.t.l. p. 174.

F.R. 1941-28
HARVEST IN BRITANNY
On the back: BUNCH OF FLOWERS IN FRONT
OF A WINDOW OVERLOOKING THE SEA
T. H. 0.73; W. 0.92.
S.D.b.g.: P. Gauguin, 88.
(Wildenstein 269 and 292).
Paul Jamot bequest, 1941.
Cat. impr. 130 — S.A.I. 900 — C.P.t.l. p. 172.

F.R. 1938-42
LES ALYSCAMPS, Arles.
T. H. 0.915; W. 0.725.
S.D.b.g.: P. Gauguin, 88.
(Wildenstein 307).
Presented by Countess Vitali in memory of her
brother, Vicomte Guy du Cholet, 1923. On deposit
from the Museum of Decorative Arts; entered the
Louvre Museum in 1938.
Cat. impr. 131 — S.A.I. 899 — C.P.t.l. p. 172.

F.R. 1959-8
SCHUFFENECKER'S STUDIO, also known as
THE SCHUFFENECKER FAMILY. The painter
Emile Schuffenecker (1851-1934), with his wife
and daughters.
T. H. 0.73; W. 0.92.
S.mi-h.d.: P. Go. Dedicated D.b.d. Souvenir
for good old Schuffenecker, 1889.
(Wildenstein 313).
Ex-Matsukata collection. Entered the Louvre
Museum 1959, in accordance with the Peace
Treaty with Japan.
Cat. impr. 132 — S.A.I. 901 — C.P.t.l. p. 174.

F.R. 1951-6
YELLOW HAYSTACKS, also known as THE BLOND
HARVEST
T. H. 0.735; W. 0.925.
S.D.b.d.: P. Gauguin, 89.
(Wildenstein 351).
Presented by Mme Huc de Monfreid, 1951; entered
in 1968.
C.P.t.l. p. 173.

F.R. 1959-7
STILL-LIFE WITH FAN
T. H. 0.50; W. 0.61.
S.b.d.: P. Gauguin.
Painted ap. 1889.
(Wildenstein 377).
Ex-Matsukata collection. Entered the Louvre
Museum in 1959, in accordance with the Peace
Treaty with Japan.
Cat. impr. 134 — S.A.I. 903 — C.P.t.l. p. 173.

F.R. 2617
"LA BELLE ANGÈLE"
(Mme Satre, hotel-keeper at Pont-Aven).
T.H. 0.92; W. 0.73.
S.D.b.g.: P. Gauguin, 89. Inscr.b.g.: La belle Angèle.
(Wildenstein 315).
Presented by Ambroise Vollard, 1927.
Cat. impr. 133 — S.A.I. 902 — C.P.t.l. p. 172.

F.R. 2765
WOMEN FROM TAHITI also known as ON THE
BEACH
T. H. 0.690; W. 0.915.
S.D.b.d.: P. Gauguin, 91.
(Wildenstein 434).
Bequeathed by Vicomte Guy du Cholet, 1923.
Cat. impr. 135 — S.A.I. 904 — C.P.t.l. p. 172.

F.R. 1954-27
THE MEAL
T. H.0.73; W. 0.92.
S.D.b.d.: P. Gauguin 91.
(Wildenstein 427).
Presented by M. and Mme André Meyer, with
reservation of usufruct, 1954. Usufruct
abandoned, 1975.

F.R. 1961-6
AREAREA (PLEASANTERIES)
T. H. 0.75; W. 0.94.
Inscr. S.d.b.d.: Arearea. P. Gauguin, 92.
(Wildenstein 468).
Bequeathed by M. and Mme Frédéric Lung, 1961.
C.P.t.l. p. 174.

F.R. 1958-11
FLORAL AND PLANT DECORATIONS
Glass. H. 1.05; W. 0.75.
Inscr. B.d.: Nave Nave.
Painted in 1893.
Glass panes decorating the artist's studio in the rue
Vercingétorix, Paris.
(Wildenstein 510).
Presented by Mrs. Harold English, 1958.
Cat. impr. 138a — S.A.I. 906 — C.P.t.l. p. 173.

F.R. 158-12
LANDSCAPE WITH A TAHITIAN GIRL
Glass. H. 1.16; W. 0.75.
D.b.d. 93.
Glass panes decorating the artist's studio,
rue Vercingétorix, Paris.
(Wildenstein 511).
Presented by Mrs. Harold English, 1958.
Cat. impr. 135 b — S.A.I. 905 — C.P.t.l. p. 173.

F.R. 1966-7
SELF-PORTRAIT
On the back: PORTRAIT OF WILLIAM MOLARD,
Swedish composer, (d.1936).
T.H. 0.46; W. 0.38.

S.h.g. on back: P. Go.
Painted ap. 1893-94.
(Wildenstein 506 and 507).
Acquired in 1966.
C.P.t.l. p. 174.

F.R. 1959-6
BRETON LANDSCAPE (LE MOULIN DAVID)
T. H. 0.73; W. 0.92.
S.D.b.d.: 94. P. Gauguin.
(Wildenstein 528).
Ex-collection Matsukata. Entered the Louvre
Museum in 1959, in accordance with the Peace
Treaty with Japan.
Cat. impr. 136 — S.A.I. 907 — C.P.t.l. p. 173.

F.R. 1952-29
BRETON VILLAGE UNDER SNOW
T. H. 0.62; W. 0.87.
Certainly painted in 1894. Discovered in his hut
after his death.
(Wildenstein 525).
Acquired in 1952 with deferred payments from
an anonymous donation from Canada.
Cat. impr. 137 — S.A.I. 908 — C.P.t.l. p. 173.

F.R. 1973-17
PEASANT-WOMEN FROM BRITANNY
T. H. 0.66; W. 0.925.
S.D.b.g.: P. Gauguin 94.
(Wildenstein 521).
M. and R. Kaganovitch donation, 1973.

F.R. 1951-7
SELF-PORTRAIT
T. H. 0.405; W. 0.320.
Dedicated and S.b.d.: to my friend Daniel,
P. Gauguin.
Painted in 1896.
(Wildenstein 556).
Presented by Mme Huc de Monfried, 1951;
entered the Louvre Museum, 1968.
C.P.t.l. p. 173.

F.R. 1959-5
VAIRUMATI
T. H. 0.73; W. 0.94.
Inscr. S.D.b.g.: Vairumati, 99, P. Gauguin.
(Wildenstein 559).
Ex-collection Matsukata. Entered the Louvre
Museum in 1959, in accordance with the Peace
Treaty with Japan.
Cat. impr. 139 — S.A.I. 909 — C.P.t.l. p. 173.

F.R. 2616
THE WHITE HORSE
T. H. 1.404; W. 0.915.
S.D.b.m.: P. Gauguin, 98.
(Wildenstein 571).
Acquired in 1927.
Cat. impr. 139 — S.A.I. 910 — C.P.t.l. p. 172.

F.R. 1944-2
"ET L'OR DE LEURS CORPS"
T. H. 0.67; W. 0.76.
Inscr. S.D.b.d.: And their golden bodies.
P. Gauguin, 1901.
(Wildenstein 596).
Acquired in 1944.
Cat. impr. 140 — S.A.I. 911 — C.P.t.l. p. 173.

Ceramics

Gauguin began experimenting with ceramics in
1886, but is was in 1888 that he met Chaplet, the
renovator of modern french ceramics, who taught
him the technique of glazed earthenware. The
oriental ceramics in the Guimet Museum roused
his enthusiasm. His first individual exhibition,
held in 1888 at Boussod and Valadon included
an ensemble of ceramics which attracted the
attention of Roger Marx (Revue Encyclopédique,
1891, p. 587 and seq.). In Noa-Noa, praised the
Japanese potters and in Tahiti he decorated his
garden with idols of ceramic of his own make
(J. Leymarie, Catalogue of the Gauguin Exhibition,
Orangerie, 1949, p. 81).
See: A.M. Berryer. "Concerning a Chaplet vase
decorated by Gauguin", in Le Bulletin des Musées
Royaux de Bruxelles, January 1944, pp. 13-27.

MAAO 14329[4]
SQUARE VASE WITH TWO HANDLES
H. 0.15
Signed: P. Go.
Ap. 1887.
(Gray 13).
Presented by Vollard, 1943; on deposit from
the Museum of African and Oceanic Arts.

MAAO 14329[6]
VASE - WOMAN BENEATH A TREE
H. 0.13
Signed: P. Go.
Ap. 1887.
(Gray 15).
Presented by Vollard, 1943; on deposit from
the Museum of African and Oceanic Arts.

MAAO 14329[5]
VASE WITH FOUR HANDLES - BRETON DESIGN
H. 0.17.
Signed: P. Gauguin.
(Gray 21).
Presented by Vollard, 1943; on deposit from
the Museum of African and Oceanic Arts.

MAAO 14343
Vase in the form of a tree-trunk with a squatting
Tahitian woman and two girls' heads.
H. 0.23.
Signed: P. Gauguin.
Ap. 1888.
(Gray 54).
Presented by Vollard, 1943; on deposit from
the Museum of African and Oceanic Arts.

OA 9514
SANDSTONE VASE DECORATED WITH TAHITIAN
FIGURES
H. 0.35; diameter 0.13.
(Gray 115).
Presented by David-Weill, 1938; on deposit from
the Department of Art objects.
Cat. impr. 472.

OA 9050
TOBACCO JAR
Glazed earthenware
H. 0.28; diameter 0.23.
(Gray 66)
Ex-Schuffenecker collection.
Presented by Jean Schmit to the Louvre Museum,

1938; on deposit from the Department of Art. Objects.
Cat. impr. 473.

OA 9051
CISTERN
Earthenware with green glaze
H. 0.45.
Signed: P. Gauguin.
(Gray 78).
Ex-collection Schuffenecker.
Presented by Jean Schmit to the Louvre Museum, 1938; on deposit from the Department of Art Objects.
Cat. impr. 474.

Sculptures in wood

OA 9052
DAGGER
Wooden handle sculpted with Polynesian figures and leaves. Touched up with red and green paint.
Length of handle: 0.18; total length: 0.58.
Signed: P.G.
Ap. 1890.
(Gray 90).
Ex-collection Schuffenecker.
Presented by Jean Schmit to the Louvre Museum 1938; on deposit from the Department of Art Objects.
Cat. impr. 475.

OA 9053
WALKING-STICK
Wood. Lenght: 0.86.
Sculpted knob decorated with Polynesian heads. Touched up with gold in the hollows.
On the knob, signature in red: P. Go.
Ap. 1894-94.
(Gray 104).
Ex-collection Schuffenecker.
Presented by Jean Schmit to the Louvre Museum, 1938; on deposit from the Department of Art Objects.
Cat. impr. 476.

MASK OF TEHURA
Wood. H. 0.25; W. 0.20.
Eyes painted green, flower in gold.
On the back a nude, standing female figure.
(Gray 98).
Presented with reservation of usufruct by Mme Huc de Monfreid, 1951; entered the Louvre Museum in 1968; on deposit from the Department of Art Objects.

OA 9529
IDOL WITH A PEARL
Wood. H. 0.25.
Pearl incrusted in the forehead of the seated figure.
Signed: P. Go.
First stay in Tahiti.
(Gray 94).
Presented with reservation of usufruct by Mme Huc de Monfreid, 1951; entered the Louvre Museum in 1968; on deposit from the Department of Art Objects.

OA 9540
IDOL WITH A SHELL

Wood. H. 0.27; diameter 0.04.
Halo of mother-of-pearl; incrusted bones fot teeth.
1893.
Acquired in 1951 whit the participation of Mme Huc de Monfreid; entered in 1968; on deposit from the Department of Art Objects.

MAAO 14329
WOODEN WALKING-STICK
L. 0.91.
Wood with iron ring bearing initials P. Go. in gold.
Tahiti, ap. 1893-95.
(Gray 105).
Presented by Vollard 1943; on deposit from the Museum of African and Oceanic Arts.

MAAO 14329[3]
HOLLOW CUP, MAORI STYLE
Wood. Length O.44; W. 0.26.
Signed: P.G.O.
(Gray 145).
Presented by Vollard, 1943; on deposit from the Museum of African and Oceanic Arts.

MAAO 14329[2]
HOLLOW OVAL PLATE
Wood. L. 0.46; W. 0.20.
Signed: P.G.O.
(Gray 144).
Presented by Vollard, 1943; on deposit from the Museum of African and Oceanic Arts.

MAAO 14329[1]
SAINT-ORANG
Sculpture in wood. H. 0.92.
Signed: P.G. on the back; inscription: Saint-Orang on the breast.
(Gray 137).
Presented by Vollard, 1943; on deposit from the Museum of African and Oceanic Arts.

MAAO 14811
SCULPTED FRAME
Wood. H. 0.50; W. 0.43.
In this frame there is an old photograph of a warrior from the Marquesas Isles.
(Gray 142).
Presented by Vollard, 1946; on deposit from the Museum of African and Oceanic Arts.

MAAO 8947
HEAD OF A TAHITIAN WOMAN
Drawing. Frame decorated with interlaced twigs.
B. H. 0.24; L. 0.20.
Ex-collection Vollard; presented by Ary Leblond, 1935; on deposit from the Museum of African and Oceanic Arts.
During his two stays in the South Sea Is, Gauguin bought and resold several plots of land and built, then abandoned, several huts. That at Hiva-Oa, in the Marquisas Is, was built on a plot conceded by the bishop of the archipelago. Gauguin soon quarreled with the priest, who had set out to reform the natives, and the decoration of his hut was conceived as an act of defiance. The inscriptions suggest a place of merrymaking, but in reality there was more despair than felicity in his hut. He died there, rotting with gangrene, on 8 May 1903.
Victor Ségalen, medical officer on a warship which had put in at the Marquisas a few weeks after Gauguin's death, has left a moving description of

the painter's wretched home. After the Marquisas, he visited Tahiti, where Gauguin's personal effects and sculpted panels had been transported and where he acquired the ensemble of polychrome wood carvings. The main part of this came to the Louvre Museum together with a canvas which represented—a final contradiction—a study of snow on dismal Breton cottages. (cf. F.R. 1952-29).

F.R. 2723
LINTEL OVER THE DOOR OF THE HUT AT HIVA-OA
Two womens' heads, seen in left profile, a bird, a leafy branch, frame the inscription: House of pleasure.
Wood carved by knife and coloured in polychrome.
L. 2.425; W. O. 39.
(Gray 132).
Victor Ségalen collection, acquired in 1952.
Cat. impr. 449.

F.R. 2720
HORIZONTAL PANEL USED TO DECORATE A RAFTER IN THE HUT AT HIVA-OA
Three women's heads: A Breton woman wrapped in a great, hooded cloak and two Maories, one of whom wears a flower behind her ear; a plant-stalk and a serpent accompany an incription: "Be in love, and you will be happy."
Wood carved with a knife and painted in polychrome.
L. 2.05; W. 0.40.
(Gray 132).
Victor Ségalen collection, acquiredin 1952.
A second relief of carved wood, bearing the same inscription, figured in Mme Jean Schuffenecker's collection (Boston, Museum of Fine Arts).
Cat. impr. 450.

F.R. 2722
VERTICAL PANEL FROM THE HUT IN HOVA-OA
A nude woman, seen in left profile, the right arm raised to the level of the face. On the left of the relief, a shrub with red fruit.
Wood carved with a knife and painted in polychrome.
H. 1.59; W. O. 40.
(Gray 132).
Victor Ségalen collection, acquired in 1952.
Cat. impr. 451.

F.R. 2721
VERTICAL PANEL FROM THE HUT AT HOVA-OA
A nude woman, standing, full-face, the left arm held to her head. At her feet, a tree, with brilliant red fruit, and a small dog.
Wood, carved with a knife and painted in polychrome.
H. 2.00; W. 0.395.
(Gray 132).
Victor Ségalen collection; acquired in 1952.
Cat. impr. 452.

MAAO 14392
MASK OF A TAHITIAN MAN
Bronze. H. 0.25.
Ap. 1893.
(Gray 110).
Presented by Vollard; on deposit from the Museum of African and Oceanic Arts.

F.R. 1952-30
GAUGUIN'S PALETTE
B. H. 0.32; W. O. 0.44.
Acquired in 1952.

GOENEUTTE Norbert
Paris, 1854 - Auvers-sur-Oise, 1894.

F.R. 757
DR. PAUL GACHET (1828-1894)
B. H. 0.35; W. 0.27.
Dedicated S.D.b.g.: To my friend Dr. Gachet.
Norbert Goeneutte, Paris, 1891.
Presented by Dr. Gachet, 1892.
Cat. impr. 141 — S.A.I. 980 — C.P.t.l. p. 185.

GONZALÈS Eva
Paris, 1849-1883.

F.R. 2643
A BOX AT THE ITALIENS THEATRE
T. H. 0.98; W. 1.30.
S.b.g.: Eva Gonzalès.
Refused at the 1874 Salon. Exhibited at
the 1879 Salon. Presented by Jean Guérard, son
of the artist, 1927.
Cat. impr. 158 — S.A.I. 982 — C.P.t.l. p. 185.

GUILLAUMIN Armand
Paris, 1841-1927.

F.R. 1954-10
A LANE: STUDY IN SNOW
T. H. 0.66; W. 0.55.
S.D.b.d.: A. Guillaumin, X. 69.
(Serret-Fabiani 5).
Presented by Paul Gachet, 1954.
Cat. impr. 163 — S.A.I. 1028 — C.P.t.l. p. 196.

F.R. 1954-11
CANAL-BOATS ON THE SEINE AT BERCY
T.H. 0.51; W. O.73.
S.D.b.g.: A. Guillaumin, 1871.
(Serret-Fabiani 11).
Presented by Paul Gachet, 1954.
Cat. imp. 164 — S.A.I. 1029 — C.P.t.l. p. 196.

F.R. 1954-9
STILL-LIFE WITH FLOWERS, CHINA AND BOOKS
T. H. 0.325; W. 0.460.
S.D.b.d.: A. Guillaumin, 7.72.
(Serret-Fabiani 14).
Presented by Paul Gachet, 1954.
Cat. impr. 165 — S.A.I. 1030 — C.P.t.l. p. 196.

F.R. 1951-34
SUNSET OVER IVRY
T. H. 0.65; W. 0.81.
S.b.g.: A. Guillaumin.
Painted in 1873.
(Serret-Fabiani 20).
Presented by Paul Gachet, 1951.
Cat. impr. 166 — S.A.I. 1031 — C.P.t.l. p. 196.

F.R. 1937-29
PARIS, QUAI DE BERCY, STUDY IN SNOW
T. H. 0.505; W. 0.612.
S.b.d.: A. Guillaumin.
Painted ap. 1873.
(Serret-Fabiani 29).
Antonin Personnaz bequest, 1937.
Cat. impr. 176 — S.A.I. 1041 — C.P.t.l. p. 195.

F.R. 1949-18
SELF-PORTRAIT

T. H. 0.73, W. 0.60.
Painted ap. 1875.
(Serret-Fabiani 39).
Presented by Paul and Marguerite Gachet, 1949.
Cat. impr. 169 — S.A.I. 1034 — C.P.t.l. p. 196.

F.R. 1937-28
PLACE VALHUBERT, in Paris
T. H. 0.645; W. 0.810.
S.b.d.: A. Guillaumin.
Painted ap. 1875.
(Serret-Fabiani 43).
Antonin Personnaz bequest, 1937.
Cat. impr. 168 — S.A.I. 1033 — C.P.t.l. p. 195.

F.R. 1951-35
NUDE WOMAN, RECLINING
T. H. 0.49; W. 0.65.
S.b.d.: A. Guillaumin.
Painted ap. 1877.
(Serret-Fabiani 51).
Presented by Paul Gachet, 1951.
Cat. impr. 167 — S.A.I. 1032 — C.P.t.l. p. 196.

F.R. 1937-26
LANDSCAPE OF PLAIN (Ile-de-France)
T. H. 0.540; W. 0.655.
S.b.d.: A. Guillaumin.
Painted ap. 1878.
(Serret-Fabiani 62).
Antonin Personnaz bequest, 1937.
Cat. impr. 177 — S.A.I. 1042 — C.P.t.l. p. 195.

F.R. 1937-34
THE HARBOUR AT CHARENTON
T. H. 0.61; W. 1.00.
S.D.b.d.: A. Guillaumin, 78.
(Serret-Fabiani 69).
Antonin Personnaz bequest, 1937.
Cat. impr. 170 — S.A.I. 1035 — C.P.t.l. p. 196.

F.R. 1937-33
FISHERMEN
T. H. 0.85; W. 0.66.
S.b.d.: Guillaumin.
Painted ap. 1885.
Serret-Fabiani 122).
Antonin Personnaz bequest, 1937.
Cat. impr. 172 — S.A.I. 1037 — C.P.t.l. p. 196.

F.R. 1937-31
BEND OF A ROAD AFTER RAIN. Road to Damiette?
T. H. 0.605; W. 0.738.
S.b.d.: Guillaumin.
Painted ap. 1887.
Antonin Personnaz bequest, 1937.
Cat. impr. 175 — S.A.I. 1040 — C.P.t.l. p. 196.

F.R. 1937-30
LANDSCAPE IN NORMANDY: APPLE-TREES
T. H. 0.60; W. 1.00.
S.b.g.: Guillaumin.
Painted ap. 1887.
(Serret-Fabiani 114).
Antonin Personnaz bequest, 1937.
Cat. impr. 178 — S.A.I. 1043 — C.P.t.l. p. 195.

F.R. 1937-32
VIEW OF AGAY (Var). Cape Dramont
T. H. 0.73; W. 0.92.
S.b.d.: Guillaumin.
Inscription on back: April, May 95, Cape Dramont,
9 a.m.

(Serret-Fabiani 340).
Antonin Personnaz bequest, 1937.
Cat. impr. 174 — S.A.I. 1039 — C.P.t.l. p. 196.

F.R. 1937-27
VIEW OF HOLLAND. SAILING SHIPS
T. H. 0.60; W. 0.73.
S.b.g.: Guillaumin.
Painted in May-June 1904.
(Serret-Fabiani 603).
Antonin Personnaz bequest, 1937.
Cat. impr. 179 — S.A.I. 1044 — C.P.t.l. p. 195.

HELLEU Paul
Vannes, 1859 - Paris 1927

F.R. 1975-22
THE YACHT MEREUS LAID UP AT COWES
T. H. 0.65; W. 0.81.
S.b.d. (twice): Helleu.
Painted ap. 1900.
Presented by Mme Howard-Johnston, née Helleu,
1975.

JONGKIND Johan-Barthold
Latrop (Holland), 1819 - Saint-Egrève (Isère),
1891.

F.R. 1703
RUINS OF ROSEMONT CASTLE
T. H. 0.340; W. 0.565.
S.D.b.g.: Jongkind, 1861.
"Salon des refusés", 1863.
(Hefting 216).
Etienne Moreau-Nélaton donation, 1907.
Brière M. 70 — Cat. impr. 180 — S.A.I. 1139.
C.P.t.l. p. 217.

F.R. 1972-20
THE SEINE AND NOTRE-DAME DE PARIS
T. H. 0.42; W. 0.565.
S.D.b.g.: Jongkind 1864.
(Hefting 291).
Eduardo Mollard bequest, 1972.

F.R. 1990
IN HOLLAND, BOATS BESIDE THE MILL
T. H. 0.525; W. 0.813.
S.D.b.g.: Jongkind, 1868.
(Hefting 455).
Camondo bequest, 1911.
Brière CA. 172 — Cat. impr. 181 — S.A.I. 1140.
C.P.t.l. p. 217.

F.R. 1291
THE MEUSE AT DORDRECHT
T. H. 0.250; W. 0.328.
S.D.b.g.: Jongkind, 1870.
Georges Lutz bequest, 1902.
C.P.t.l. p. 217.

F.R. 1972-21
RUE DE L'ABBÉ-DE-L'ÉPÉE
T. H. 0.47; W. 0.335.
S.D.b.g.: Jongkind, 1872.
(Hefting 580).
Eduardo Mollard bequest, 1972.

LEBOURG Charles-Albert
Montfort-sur-Risle (Eure), 1849 - Rouen, 1928.

F.R. 1937-40
THE HARBOUR AT ALGIERS
T. H. 0.312; W. 0.470.
S.D.b.g.: A. Lebourg, Alger, 76.
(Bénédite 15).
Antonin Personnaz bequest, 1937.
Cat. impr. 183 — S.A.I. 1157 — C.P.t.l. p. 230.

F.R. 3795
ROAD BESIDE THE SEINE, AT NEUILLY,
IN WINTER
T. H. 0.50; W. 0.73.
S.b.g.: Albert Lebourg, Neuilly-sur-Seine.
Painted ap. 1888.
(Bénédite 963).
Etienne Moreau-Nélaton, 1927.
Cat. impr. 182 — S.A.I. 1156 — C.P.t.l. p. 230.

F.R. 3793
BY THE RIVER AIN
T. H. 0.500; W. 0.655.
S.b.g.: A. Lebourg.
Painted in 1897.
(Bénédite 5).
Etienne Moreau-Nélaton bequest, 1927.
Cat. impr. 185 — S.A.I. 1159 — C.P.t.l. p. 230.

INV. 20052
THE LOCK AT LA MONNAIE, IN PARIS
T. H. 0,815; W. 1.115.
S.b.d.: A. Lebourg.
(Bénédite p. 301).
Acquired in 1918.
Cat. impr. 184 — S.A.I. 1158 — C.P.t.l. p. 230.

F.R. 1973-6
SNOW AT PONT-DU-CHATEAU
T. H. 0.40; W. 0.735.
S. b.g. Albert (illegible) Lebourg.
Attributed by the Ministry of Economy and Finance,
1974.

F.R. 1973-4
STEAM-TUGS AT ROUEN
T. H. 0.50; W. 0.735.
S.D.b.g.: A. Lebourg 1903.
(Bénédite 1371).
Attributed by the Ministry of Economy and Finance.

LÉPINE Stanislas
Caen, 1836 - Paris, 1892.

F.R. 1938-5
THE PORT AT CAEN
T. H. 0.723; W. 0.915.
S.b.g.: S. Lépine.
Painted ap. 1859.
Presented by Paul Jamot, 1938.
Cat. impr. 186 — S.A.I. 1171 — C.P.t.l. p. 240.

F.R. 2672
THE ARTIST'S SON
B. H. 0.247; W. 0.138.
Presented by M. Lépine, the artist's grandson, 1928.
Cat. impr. 188 — S.A.I. 1173 — C.P.t.l. p. 240.

F.R. 1972-22
LIGHTER ALONGSIDE THE QUAY
T. H. 0.37; W. 0.54.
S.b.g.: S. Lépine.
Eduardo Mollard bequest, 1972.

F.R. 1972-23
THE SEINE AT CHARENTON
T. H. 0.38; W. 0.60.
S.b.g. S. Lépine.
Eduardo Mollard bequest, 1972.

F.R. 1972-24
MONTMARTRE, RUE SAINT-VINCENT
T. H. 0.675; W. 0.485.
S.b.g.: S. Lépine.
Eduardo Mollard bequest, 1972.

F.R. 1972-25
THE EMBANKMENTS OF THE SEINE, PONT
MARIE
T. H. 0.30; W. 0.50.
S.D.b.g.: S. Lépine 68.
Eduardo Mollard bequest, 1972.

F.R. 1972-26
LANDSCAPE
T. H. 0.30; W. 0.585.
S.D.b.g.: S. Lépine 69.
Eduardo Mollard bequest, 1972.

F.R. 869
THE APPLE-MARKET
T. H. 0.35; W. 0.27.
1889 Salon. Acquired in 1893.
Cat. impr. 187 — S.A.I. 1172 — C.P.t.l. p. 240.

LÉVY Michel

F.R. 1971-10
PORTRAIT OF GUERBOIS (1824-1891),
Landlord of the Café Guerbois.
T. H. 0.46; W. 0.38.
S.h.d.: Michel Lévy.
Dedicated on the back: Dedicated to my
grand-daughter Mademoiselle Jenny Mitton.
Painted ap. 1885.
Presented by M. and Mme J. Taillandier, 1971.

MANET Edouard
Paris, 1832-1883.

F.R. 1977-12
M. AND MME AUGUSTE MANET
(THE ARTIST'S PARENTS)
T. H. 1.10; W. 0.90.
S.h.g. Edouard Manet, 1860.
1861 Salon.
(Tabarant 37. Jamot et Wildenstein 37). RW I 30.
Acquired through the generosity of the Rouart-
Manet family, Mme Jeannette Veil-Picard and a
foreign donator, 1977.

F.R. 1991
LOLA DE VALENCE, Spanish dancer
T.H. 1.23; W. 0.92.
S.b.g.: Ed. Manet.
Painted in 1862.
(Tabarant 52. Jamot et Wildenstein 46). RW I 53.
Camondo bequest, 1911.
Brière CA 172 — Cat. impr. 190 — S.A.I. 1188.
C.P.t.l. p. 249.

F.R. 1668
LUNCH ON THE GRASS

T. H. 2.080; W. 2.645.
S.D.b.g.: Ed. Manet, 1863.
Salon des Refusés, 1863.
(Tabarant 66. Jamot et Wildenstein 82). RW I 69.
Etienne Moreau-Nélaton donation, 1906.
Brière M. 71 — Cat. impr. 190 — S.A.I. 1189.
C.P.t.l. p. 249.

F.R. 644
OLYMPIA
T. H. 1.305; W. 1.900.
S.D.b.g.: Ed. Manet, 1863.
1865 Salon.
(Tabarant 68. Jamot et Wildenstein 82). RW I 69.
Presented to the State by a public subscription
initiated by Claude Monet, 1890.
Brière 613 a — Cat. impr. 191 — S.A.I. 1190.
C.P.t.l. p. 249.

F.R. 1995
STEM OF WHITE PEONIES AND SECATEURS
T. H. 0.310; W. 0.465.
S.b.d. (by Mme Manet): Manet.
Painted in 1864.
(Tabarant 81. Jamot et Wildenstein 105). RW I 88.
Camondo bequest, 1911.
Brière CA. 175 — Cat. impr. 195 — S.A.I. 1194.
C.P.t.l. p. 250.

F.R. 1996
STEM OF PEONIES AND SECATEURS
T. H. 0.568; W. 0.460.
S.b.g.: M.
Painted ap. 1864.
(Tabarant 80. Jamot et Wildenstein 143). RW I 91.
Camondo bequest. 1911.
Brière CA. 176 — Cat. impr. 194 — S.A.I. 1195.
C.P.t.l. p. 250.

F.R. 1670
STILL-LIFE. FRUIT ON A TABLE
T. H. 0.450; W. 0.735.
S. d.d.: Manet.
Painted in 1864.
(Tabarant 91. Jamot et Wildenstein 100). RW I 83.
Etienne Moreau-Nélaton donation, 1906.
Brière M. 73 — Cat. impr. 192 — S.A.I. 1195.
C.P.t.l. p. 249.

F.R. 1951-9
EEL AND RED-MULLET
T. H. 0.380; W. 0.465.
S.b.g.: Manet.
Painted in 1864.
(Tabarant 89. Jamot et Wildenstein 98). RW I 81.
Presented by Dr. and Mme Albert Charpentier, 1951.
Cat. impr. 193 — S.A.I. 1191 — C.P.t.l. p. 251.

F.R. 1669
PEONIES IN A VASE WITH A SMALL PEDESTAL
T. H. 0.932; W. 0.702.
S.b.d.: Manet.
Painted in 1864.
(Tabarant 79. Jamot et Wildenstein 101). RW I 86.
Etienne Moreau-Nélaton donation, 1906.
Brière M. 72 — Cat. impr. 196 — S.A.I. 1193.
C.P.t.l. p. 249.

F.R. 3664
ANGÉLINA
T. H. 0.92; W. 0.73.
S.b.d.: Manet.

Painted in 1865.
(Tabarant 109. Jamot et Wildenstein 118).
RW I 105.
Gustave Caillebotte bequest, 1894, entered 1896.
Cat. impr. 197 — S.A.I. 1196 — C.P.t.l. p. 251.

F.R. 1976-8
BULL-FIGHT
T. H. 0.90; W. 1.105.
S.b.d.: Manet.
Painted late 1865 or early 1866.
(Tabarant 120. Jamot et Wildenstein 120).
RW I 107.
Acquired by «dation» in payment of death duties and
with the help of the society of Friends of the Louvre.

F.R. 1992
THE FIFE
T. H. 1.61; W. 0.97.
S.b.d.: Manet.
Painted in 1866.
(Tabarant 117. Jamot et Wildenstein 126).
RW I 113.
Camondo bequest, 1911.
Brière CA. 173 — Cat. impr. 198 — S.A.I. 1197.
C.P.t.l. p. 249.

F.R. 1944-17
READING. Mme Edouard Manet (1830-1906)
and her son, Léon Koella-Leenhoff (1852-1927).
T. H. 0.605; W. 0.735.
S.b.d.: Manet.
Painted ap. 1868.
(Tabarant 143. Jamot et Wildenstein 167).
RW I 136.
Bequest from Princesse Edmond de Polignac,
née Singer, 1944.
Cat. impr. 201 — S.A.I. 1200 — C.P.t.l. p. 251.

F.R. 2205
ÉMILE ZOLA (1840-1902), writer
T. H. 1.463; W. 1.140.
1868 Salon.
(Tabarant 137. Jamot et Wildenstein 146).
RW I 128.
Donation from Mme Emile Zola, with reservation
of usufruct, 1918; entered 1925.
Cat. impr. 200 — S.A.I. 119 — C.P.t.l. p. 250.

F.R. 1994
MADAME MANET AT THE PIANO. Suzanne
Leenhoff (1830-1906), the artist's wife.
T. H. 0.380; W. 0.465.
Painted ap. 1868.
(Tabarant 142. Jamot et Wildenstein 142).
RW I 131.
Camondo bequest, 1911.
Brière CA. 174 — Cat. impr. 199 — S.A.I. 1198.
C.P.t.l. p. 250.

F.R. 2772
THE BALCONY.   Berthe Morisot (1841-1895),
painter; Fanny Clausz (1846-1877), violinist; and
Antoine Guillemet (1843-1918), landscape painter.
T. H. 1.700; W. 1.245.
S.b.d.: Manet.
Painted ap. 1868-69.
1869 Salon.
(Tabarant 141. Jamot et Wildenstein 150).
RW I 134.
Gustave Caillebotte bequest, 1894; entered 1896.
Cat. impr; 202 — S.A.I. 1201 — C.P.t.l. p. 251.

F.R. 1993
MOONLIGHT OVER THE HARBOUR AT BOULOGNE
T. H. 0.82; W. 1.01.
Painted in 1869.
(Tabarant 150. Jamot et Wildenstein 159).
RW I 143.
Camondo bequest, 1911.
Brière CA. 177 — Cat. impr. 203 — S.A.I. 1202.
C.P.t.l. p. 249.

F.R. 1671
BERTHE MORISOT WITH A FAN. Berthe Morisot
(1841-1895) painter, the artist's sister-in-law.
T. H. 0.60; W. 0.45.
S. towards b.g.: Manet.
Painted in 1872.
(Tabarant 186. Jamot et Wildenstein 210).
RW I 181.
Donation Etienne Moreau-Nélation, 1906.
Brière M 74 — Cat. impr. 204 — S.A.I. 1203.
C.P.t.l. p. 249.

F.R. 1953-24
ON THE BEACH. Mme Edouard Manet (1830-
1906) and Eugène Manet (1833-1892),
the artist's wife and brother, at Berck.
T. H. 0.596; W. 0.732.
S.b.d.: Manet.
Painted during summer 1873.
Ex-collection Jacques Doucet.
(Tabarant 188. Jamot et Wildenstein 224).
RW I 188.
Donation Jean-Edouard Dubrujeaud with reserva-
tion of usufruct, 1963; entered the Louvre Museum
1970.
C.P.t.l. p. 251.

F.R. 2850
WOMAN WITH FANS. Nina de Callias (1845-
1884), musician and painter.
T. H. 1.135; W. 1.665.
S.b.d.: Manet.
Painted in 1873.
(Tabarant 224. Jamot et Wildenstein 237 bis).
RW I 208.
Presented by M. and Mme Ernest Rouart, 1930.
Cat. impr. 206 — S.A.I. 1204 — C.P.t.l. p. 251.

F.R. 1945-4
MARGUERITE DE CONFLANS, later Mme d'Angély.
T. oval; H. 0.535; W. 0.645.
Painted ap. 1875-1877.
(Tabarant 215 bis).
Bequest from Mlle d'Angély, the sitter's daughter,
1945.
Cat. impr. 205 — S.A.I. 1205 — C.P.t.l. p. 251.

F.R. 4507
MADAME MANET ON A BLUE SOFA
Pastel. H. 0.49; W. 0.60.
Bottom right: E. Manet (inscribed in pencil by
the painter's widow).
Executed ap. 1874-78.
(Tabarant 455. Jamot et Wildenstein 311).
RW II 3.
Acquired by the Louvre Museum, 1918.
Depository of the Department of Drawings.
Cat. impr. 207 — S.A.I. 1207.

F.R. 2661
STÉPHANE MALLARMÉ (1842-1898), poet.
T. H. 0.275; W. 0.360.

S.D.b.g.: Manet, 76.
(Tabarant 265. Jamot et Wildenstein 311).
RW I 249.
Acquired in 1928, with the help of the Society
of Friends of the Louvre, and of D. David-Weil.
Cat. impr. 208 — S.A.I. 1208 — C.P.t.l. p. 250.

F.R. 2637
BLONDE WOMAN WITH BARE BREASTS
T. H. 0.625; W. 0.520.
S.b.g.: E.M.
Painted ap. 1878.
(Tabarant 286. Jamot et Wildenstein 257).
RW I 176.
Etienne Moreau-Nélation bequest, 1927.
Cat. impr. 209 — S.A.I. 1209 — C.P.t.l. p. 250.

FR 1959-4
WAITRESS WITH BEER-GLASSES
T. H. 0.775; W. 0.650.
S.b.d. (by Mme Manet): E. Manet.
Right-hand part of a composition cut up by the
artist: "The café-concert at Reichshoffen." (Left-
hand part "Art the café," in the Reinhart collection
at Winterthur).
Painted in 1878-79.
(Tabarant 299. Jamot et Wildenstein 336).
RW I 311.
Ex-collection Matsukata. Entered the Louvre
Museum 1959, in accordance with the Peace
Treaty with Japan.
Cat. impr. 211 — S.A.I. 1210 — C.P.t.l. p. 251.

FR 4519
MADAME ÉMILE ZOLA
Pastel. T. H. 0.52; W. 0.44.
S.b.g.: Manet.
Ap. 1879-80.
(Tabarant 477. Jamot et Wildenstein 448).
RW II 13.
Bequeathed by Mme Emile Zola in 1918; entered
the Louvre Museum 1925.
Depository of the Department of Drawings.
Cat. impr. 212 — S.A.I. 1211.

R.F. 2641
GEORGES CLEMENCEAU (1841-1939), politician.
T. H. 0.945; W. 0.740 (unfinished and cut at the
sides and bottom).
Painted in 1879.
(Tabarant 322. Jamot et Wildenstein 372).
RW I 330.
Presented by Mrs Louisine W. Havemeyer,
New York, 1927.
Cat. impr. 213 — S.A.I. 1215 — C.P.t.l. p. 250.

R.F. 1997
LEMON
T. H. 0.14; W. 0.22.
S.b.d. (by Mme Manet): E. Manet.
Painted in 1880.
(Tabarant 370. Jamot et Wildenstein 409).
RW I 360.
Camondo bequest, 1911.
Brière CA. 178 — Cat. impr. 214 — S.A.I. 1216.
C.P.t.l. p. 250.

F.R. 1959-18
ASPARAGUS
T. H. 0.165; W. 0.215.
S.h.d.: M.
Painted in 1880.

(Tabarant 370. Jamot et Wildenstein 409).
RW I 358.
Presented by Sam Salz, 1959.
S.A.I. 1214 — C.P.t.I. p. 252.

F.R. 3392
DR. MATERNE
T. Pastel. H. 0.55; W. 0.347.
S.b.g.: E.M.
Ap. 1880.
(Tabarant 488. Jamot et Wildenstein 479).
RW II 50.
Donation Etienne Moreau-Nélaton, 1906.
Depository of the Department of Drawings.
Cat. impr. 217 — S.A.I. 1213.

M.N.R. 631
CARNATIONS AND CLEMATIS IN A CRYSTAL
VASE
T. H. 0.560; W. 0.355.
S.b.d.:Manet
Painted ap. 1882.
(Tabarant 444. Jamot et Wildenstein 506).
RW II 50.
Attributed to the Louvre Museum by the Private
Properties Office, 1951.
Cat. impr. 218 — S.A.I. 1219 — C.P.t.I. p. 252.

MONET Claude-Oscar
Paris, 1840 - Giverny (Eure), 1936.

M.N.R. 136
A CORNER OF THE STUDIO
T. H. 1.82; W. 1.27.
S.D. towards b.r.: O. Monet, 61.
(D.W.I. 6).
Attributed to the Louvre Museum by the Private
Properties Office, 1950.
Cat. impr. 220 — S.A.I. 1342 — C.P.t.I. p. 275.

M.N.R. 213
HUNT TROPHY
T. H. 1.04; W. 0.75.
S.D.b.d.: O.C. Monet 62.
(D.W.I. 10).
Attributed to the Louvre Museum by the Private
Properties Office, 1950.
Cat. impr. 221 — S.A.I. 1343 — C.P.t.I. p. 275.

F.R. 1675
STILL-LIFE
T. H. 0.24; W. 0.33.
S.b.g.: M.
Painted 1864.
(D.W.I. 14).
Etienne Moreau-Nélaton Donation, 1906.
Brière M. 75 — Cat. impr. 222 — S.A.I. 1344.
C.P.t.I. p. 270.

F.R. 1675
FARMYARD IN NORMANDY
T. H. 0.650; W. 0.813.
S.b.g.: C. Monet.
Painted ap. 1864.
(D.W.I. 56).
Bequeathed by M. and Mme Raymond Koechlin,
1931.
Cat. impr. 223 — S.A.I. 1345 — C.P.t.I. p. 274.

F.R. 1672
THE PAVÉ DE CHAILLY (Forêt de Fontainebleau).

T. H. 0.435; W. 0.590.
S.b.g.: C. Monet.
Painted in 1865.
(D.W.I. 56).
Etienne Moreau-Nélaton Donation, 1906.
Brière M. 76 — Cat. impr. 224 — S.A.I. 1346.
C.P.t.I. p. 270.

F.R. 2011
THE CART. ROAD UNDER SNOW AT HONFLEUR.
T. H. 0.650; W. 0.925.
S.b.g.: Claude Monet.
Painted ap. 1867.
(D.W.I. 50).
Camondo bequest, 1911.
Brière CA. 179 — Cat. impr. 225 — S.A.I. 1347.
C.P.t.I. p. 272.

F.R. 1957-7
FRAGMENT OF "LUNCH ON THE GRASS"
(left-hand part).
T. H. 4.18; W. 1.50.
Painted in 1865-66.
(D.W.I. 63a).
Presented by Georges Wildenstein, 1957.
Cat. impr. 226 — S.A.I. 1348 — C.P.t.I. p. 275.

M.N.R. 216
GARDEN IN FLOWER
T. H. 0.65; W. 0.54.
S.b.g.: Claude Monet.
Painted ap. 1866.
(D.W.I. 69).
Attributed to the Louvre Museum by the Private
Properties Office, 1950.
Cat. impr. 227 — S.A.I. 1349 — C.P.t.I. p. 275.

F.R. 2773
WOMEN IN THE GARDEN
T. H. 2.55; W. 2.05.
S.b.d.: Claude Monet.
(D.W.I. 67).
Acquired in 1921.
Cat. impr. 228 — S.A.I. 1351 — C.P.t.I. p. 273.

F.R. 1951-20
MADAME GAUDIBERT, wife of a collector
at Le Havre.
T. H. 2.170; W. 1.385.
S.D.b.d.: Claude Monet, 1868.
(D.W.I. 121).
Acquired with deferred payments from an
anonymous gift from Canada, 1951.
Cat. impr. 229 — S.A.I. 1352 — C.P.t.I. p. 275.

F.R. 1678
HIGH SEAS AT ETRETAT
T. H. 0.66; W. 1.31.
S.b.g.: Claude Monet.
Painted ap. 1868.
(D.W.I. 127).
Etienne Moreau-Nélaton donation, 1906.
Brière M. 83 — Cat. impr. 239 — S.A.I. 1361 —
C.P.t.I. p. 270.

F.R. 1947-30
HOTEL DES ROCHES NOIRES AT TROUVILLE
T. H. 0.811; W. 0.583.
S.D.b.d.: Claude Monet 1870.
(D.W.I. 155).
Presented by M. Jacques Laroche with
reservation of usufruct 1947, entered in 1976.

M.N.R. 218
THE COUNTRY TRAIN
T. H. 0.50; W. 0.65.
S.b.g.: Claude Monet.
Painted ap. 1870-71.
(D.W.I. 153).
Attributed to the Louvre Museum by the Private
Properties Office, 1950.
Cat. impr. 230 — S.A.I. 1350 — C.P.t.I. p. 276.

F.R. 1677
FISH-CART AT ANCHOR
T. H. 0.48; W. 0.75.
S.b.d.: Claude Monet.
Painted ap. 1871.
(D.W.I. 207).
Etienne Moreau-Nélaton donation, 1906.
Brière M 78 — Cat. impr. 232 — S.A.I. 1354 —
C.P.t.I. p. 270.

F.R. 3665
MADAME MONET ON THE SOFA.
Camille Doncieux (1847-1879), the artist's first
wife.
T. H. 0.48; W. 0.75.
S.b.g.: Claude Monet.
Painted ap. 1871.
(D.W.I. 163).
Bequeathed by M. and Mme Raymond Koechlin,
1931.
Cat. impr. 233 — S.A.I. 1355 — C.P.t.I. p. 273.

F.R. 1637
ZAANDAM (Holland).
T. H. 0.478; W. 0.730.
S.b.g.: Claude Monet.
Painted in 1871.
(DWI 183).
Etienne Moreau-Nélaton donation, 1906.
Brière M. 77 — Cat. impr. 231 — S.A.I. 1353 —
C.P.t.I. p. 270.

F.R. 1961-4
ARGENTEUIL
T. H. 0.50; W. 0.65.
S.D.b.g.: Claude Monet, 72.
(D.W.I. 230).
Bequeathed by M. and Mme Frédéric Lung, 1961.
C.P.t.I. p. 275.

F.R. 2778
REGATTA AT ARGENTEUIL
T. H. 0.48; W. 0.75.
S.b.d.: Claude Monet.
Painted ap. 1872.
(D.W.I. 233).
Gustave Caillebotte bequest, 1894; entered 1896.
Cat. impr. 234 — S.A.I. 1356 — C.P.t.I. p. 273.

M.N.R. 855
LANDSCAPE.. VIEW OF THE PLAIN AT ARGENTEUIL
T. H. 0.53; W. 0.72.
S.D.b.d.: 72. Claude Monet.
(D.W.I. 220).
Attributed to the Louvre Museum by the Private
Properties Office, 1951.
Cat. impr. 235 — S.A.I. 1357 — C.P.t.I. p. 276.

F.R. 1674
QUARRIES AT SAINT-DENIS
T. H. 0.61; W. 0.81.
S.D.b.g.: 72. Claude Monet.

(D.W.I. 237)
Etienne Moreau-Nélaton donation, 1906.
Brière M. 79 — Cat. impr. 237 — S.A.I. 1359 —
C.P.t.I. p. 270.

F.R. 1937-43
THE STREAM AT ROBEC, near Rouen.
T. H. 0.50; W. 0.65.
S.D.b.d.: Claude Monet, 72.
Antonin Personnaz bequest, 1937.
Cat. impr. 236 — S.A.I. 1358 — C.P.t.I. p. 274.

THE RAILWAY-BRIDGE AT ARGENTEUIL
(Val-d'Oise)
T. H. 0.54; W. 0.71.
S.b.d.: Claude Monet.
Painted ap. 1873.
(D.W.I. 319).
Etienne Moreau-Nélaton donation, 1906.
Brière M. 82 — Cat. impr. 241 — S.A.I. 1363 —
C.P.t.I. p. 270.

F.R. 1680
RESTING UNDER THE LILACS
T. H. 0.500; W. 0.657.
S.b.d.: Claude Monet.
Painted ap. 1873.
(D.W.I. 203).
Brière M. 81 — Cat. impr. 242 — S.A.I. 1364 —
C.P.t.I. p. 270.

F.R. 1676
WILD POPPIES
T. H. 0.50; W. 0.65.
S.D.b.g.: Claude Monet, 73.
(D.W.I. 274).
Etienne Moreau-Nélaton donation, 1906.
Brière M. 80 — Cat. impr. 238 — S.A.I. 1360 —
C.P.t.I. p. 270.

F.R. 1951-13
THE SEINE AT ARGENTEUIL
T. H. 0.503; W. 0.610.
S.b.d.: Claude Monet.
Painted in 1873.
(D.W.I. 198).
Presented by Dr. and Mme Albert Charpentier,
1951.
Cat. impr. 242a — S.A.I. 1366 — C.P.t.I. p. 274.

F.R. 2437
PLEASURE-BOATS
T. H. 0.49; W. 0.65.
S.b.g.: Claude Monet.
Painted ap. 1873.
(D.W.I. 229).
Presented by Ernest May with reservation of
usufruct, 1923; entered 1926.
Cat. impr. 243 — S.A.I. 1362 — C.P.t.I. p. 272.

F.R. 2774
THE LUNCH
T. H. 1.60; W. 2.01.
S.b.d.: Claude Monet.
Painted ap. 1873.
(D.W.I. 285).
Gustave Caillebotte bequest, 1894; entered 1896.
Cat. impr. 243 — S.A.I. 1365 — C.P.t.I. p. 273.

F.R. 1937-41
THE BRIDGE AT ARGENTEUIL
T. H. 0.605; W. 0.800.

S.D.b.d.: Claude Monet, 74.
(D.W.I. 311).
Antonin Personnaz bequest, 1937
Cat. impr. 245 — S.A.I. 1368 — C.P.t.I. p. 274.

F.R. 2008
BOATS. REGATTA AT ARGENTEUIL
T. H. 0.60; W. 1.00.
S.b.d.: Cl. Monet.
Painted in 1874.
(D.W.I. 399).
Camondo bequest, 1911.
Brière CA. 180 — Cat. impr. 244 — S.A.I. 1367 —
C.P.t.I. p. 271.

F.R. 2776
INTERIOR OF AN APARTMENT
T. H. 0.815; W. 0.605.
S.D.b.m.: Claude Monet, 75.
(D.W.I. 365).
Gustave Caillebotte bequest, 1894; entered 1896.
Cat. impr. 247 — S.A.I. 1370 — C.P.t.I. p. 273.

F.R. 2705
LES TUILERIES. Study
T. H. 0.50; W. 0.75.
S.D.b.g.: Claude Monet, 75.
(D.W.I. 403).
Gustave Caillebotte bequest, 1894; entered 1896.
Cat. impr. 246 — S.A.I. 1370 — C.P.t.I. p. 272.

F.R. 2010
THE DOCK AT ARGENTEUIL
T. H. 0.600; W. 0.805.
S.b.g.: Claude Monet.
Painted in 1875.
(D.W.I. 225).
Camondo bequest, 1911.
Brière CA. 181 — Cat. impr. 248 — S.A.I. 1371.

F.R. 1944-18
TURKEY-COCKS
T. H. 1.744; W. 1.725.
S.D.b.d.: Claude Monet, 77.
(D.W.I. 416).
Bequeathed by Princess Edmond de Polignac,
née Singer, 1944.
Cat. impr. 250 — S.A.I. 1373 — C.P.t.I. p. 274.

F.R. 2775
GARE SAINT-LAZARE
T. H. 0.755; W. 1.040.
S.D.b.d.: 1877, Claude Monet.
(D.W.I. 438).
Gustave Caillebotte bequest, 1894; entered 1896.
Cat. impr. 249 — S.A.I. 1372 — C.P.t.I. p. 273.

F.R. 1951-36
CHRYSANTHEMUM
T. H. 0.545; W. 0.650.
S.b.g.: Claude Monet. D.b.d.: 1878.
(D.W.I. 492).
Presented by Paul Gachet, 1951.
Cat. impr. 251 — S.A.I. 1374 — C.P.t.I. p. 275.

F.R. 3755
THE CHURCH AT VÉTHEUIL. SNOW
T. H. 0.653; W. 0.71.
S.b.g.: Claude Monet.
Painted during the winter 1878-79.
(D.W.I. 506).
Gustave Caillebotte bequest, 1894; entered 1896.
Cat. impr. 252 — S.A.I. 1375 — C.P.t.I. p. 274.

F.R. 1973-18
THE CHURCH AT VÉTHEUIL
T. H. 0.653; W. 0.505.
S.b.g.: Claude Monet; D.b.d.: 1879.
(D.W.I. 505).
M. and R. Kaganovitch donation, 1973.

F.R. 1963-3
CAMILLE ON HER DEATH-BED
Camille Doncieux (1847-1879), the artist's first
wife.
T. H. 0.90; W. 0.68.
Stamp b.d.: Claude Monet.
Painted in 1879.
(D.W.I. 543).
Presented by Mme Katia Granoff, 1963.
C.P.t.I. p. 275.

F.R. 1998
THE SEINE AT VÉTHEUIL (Val-d'Oise).
STUDY OF SUN AFTER RAIN
T. H. 0.60; W. 0.81.
S.D.b.d.: Claude Monet, 79.
(D.W.I. 528).
Camondo bequest, 1911.
Brière CA. 182 — Cat. impr. 254 — S.A.I. 1377 —
C.P.t.I. p. 270.

F.R. 2639
LANDSCAPE AT VÉTHEUIL
T. H. 0.600; W. 0.735.
S.D.b.d.: Claude Monet, 79.
Legs Etienne Moreau-Nélaton, 1927.
Cat. impr. 253 — S.A.I. 1376 — C.P.t.I. p. 272.

F.R. 1937-3
THE SEINE AT VÉTHEUIL
T.H. 0.435; W. 0.705.
S.b.d.: Cl. M.
Painted ap. 1879-82.
(D.W.I. 532).
Presented by Dr. and Mme Albert Charpentier,
1937.
Cat. impr. 255 — S.A.I. 1387 — C.P.t.I. p. 172.

F.R. 2706
HOAR-FROST
T. H. 0.61; W. 1.00.
S.D.b.d.: 1880, Claude Monet.
(D.W.I. 555).
Gustave Caillebotte bequest, 1894; entered 1896.
Cat. impr. 256 — S.A.I. 1378 — C.P.t.I. p. 272.

F.R. 1965-10
BREAK-UP ON THE SEINE
T. H. 0.60; W. 1.00.
S.D.b.d.: Claude Monet, 1880.
(D.W.I. 567).
Presented by Baroness Eva Gebhard-Gourgaud,
1965.
C.P.t.I. p. 275.

F.R. 1937-42
ETRETAT
T. H. 0.66; W. 0.81.
S.D.b.d.: Claude Monet, 83.
Antonin Personnaz bequest, 1937.
Cat. impr. 257 — S.A.I. 1380 — C.P.t.I. p. 274.

F.R. 2009
THE SEINE AT PORT-VILLEZ (Yvelines)
T. H. 0.65; W. 0.92.

S.b.g.: Claude Monet.
Painted in 1883.
Camondo bequest, 1911.
Brière CA. 183 — Cat. impr. 258 — S.A.I. 1381 —
C.P.t.l. p. 272.

F.R. 1944-19
TULIP-FIELDS IN HOLLAND
T. H. 0.655; W. 0.815.
S.D.b.g.: Claude Monet, 86.
Bequeathed by Princess Edmond de Polignac,
née Singer, 1944.
Cat. impr. 261 — S.A.I. 1384 — C.P.t.l. p. 274.

F.R. 2777
ROCKS AT BELLE-ILE
T. H. 0.65; W. 0.815.
S.D.b.d.: Claude Monet, 86.
Gustave Caillebotte bequest, 1894; entered 1896.
Cat. impr. 259 — S.A.I. 1382 — C.P.t.l. p. 273.

F.R. 3163
STORM ON THE BELLE-ILE COAST
T. H. 0.650; W. 0.815.
S.D.b.g.: Claude Monet, 86.
Bequeathed by Gaston Migeon, 1931.
Cat. impr. 260 — S.A.I. 1383 — C.P.t.l. p. 273.

F.R. 2620.
WOMAN WITH PARASOL TURNED TO
THE RIGHT. Suzanne Hoschedé (1899), daughter
of the artist's second wife.
T. H. 1.31; W. 0.88.
S.D.b.d.: Claude Monet, 86.
Presented by Michel Monet, the artist's son, 1927.
Cat. impr. 262 — S.A.I. 1385 — C.P.t.l. p. 272.

F.R. 2621
WOMAN WITH PARASOL TURNED TO THE LEFT.
Suzanne Hoschedé (1899), daughter of the artist's
second wife.
T. H. 1.31; W. 0.88.
S.D.b.g.: Claude Monet, 86.
Presented by Michel Monet, the artist's son, 1927.
Cat. impr. 263 — S.A.I. 1386 — C.P.t.l. p. 272.

F.R. 1944-20
BOAT AT GIVERNY
The daughters of Mme Hoschedé, the artist's
second wife.
T. H. 0.96; W. 1.31.
S.b.d.: Claude Monet.
Painted ap. 1887.
Bequeathed by Princess Edmond de Polignac,
née Singer, 1944.
Cat. impr. 264 — S.A.I. 1387 — C.P.t.l. p. 274.

F.R. 1975-3
HAYSTACKS
T. H. 0.605; W. 1.00.
S.D.b.g.: Claude Monet 91.
Acquired in 1975.

F.R. 1999
ROUEN CATHEDRAL. THE PORTAL.
CLOUDY WEATHER
T. H. 1.00; W. 0.65.
S.D.b.g.: Claude Monet, 94.
Camondo bequest, 1911.
Brière CA. 184 — Cat. impr. 265 — S.A.I. 1388 —
C.P.t.l. p. 271.

F.R. 2000
ROUEN CATHEDRAL. THE PORTAL. MORNING

SUN. HARMONY IN BLUE.
T. H. 0.91; W. 0.63.
S.D.b.d.: Claude Monet, 94.
Camondo bequest, 1911.
Brière CA. 185 — Cat. impr. 266 — S.A.I. 1389 —
C.P.t.l. p. 271.

F.R. 2001
ROUEN CATHEDRAL. THE PORTAL AND SAINT-
ROMAN TOWER. MORNING STUDY. HARMONY
IN WHITE.
T. H. 1.06; W. 0.73.
S.D.b.g.: Claude Monet, 94.
Camondo bequest, 1911.
Brière CA. 186 — Cat. impr. 267 — S.A.I. 1391.

F.R. 2002
ROUEN CATHEDRAL. THE PORTAL AND
SAINT-ROMAN TOWER. FULL SUN. HARMONY
IN BLUE AND GOLD.
T. H. 1.07; W. 0.73.
S.D.b.g.: Claude Monet, 94.
Camondo bequest, 1911.
Brière CA. 187 — Cat. impr. 268 — S.A.I. 1390.
C.P.t.l. p. 271.

F.R. 2779
ROUEN CATHEDRAL. HARMONY IN BROWN
T. H. 1.07; W. 0.73.
S.D.b.g.: Claude Monet, 94.
Acquired 1907.
Cat. impr. 269 — S.A.I. 1392 — C.P.t.l. p. 273.

F.R. 1967-7
MOUNT KOLSAAS IN NORWAY
T. H. 0.655; W. 1.00.
Cachet b.d.: Claude Monet.
Painted in 1895.
Acquired 1967.
C.P.t.l. p. 275.

F.R. 2003
BRANCH OF THE SEINE NEAR GIVERNY
T. H. 0.750; W. 0.925.
S.D.b.g.: Claude Monet, 97.
Camondo bequest, 1911.
Brière CA. 188 — Cat. impr. 270 — S.A.I. 1393 —
C.P.t.l. p. 271.

F.R. 2004
THE WATER-LILY POND. HARMONY IN GREEN
T. H. 0.890; W. 0.935.
S.D.b.g.: Claude Monet, 99.
Camondo bequest, 1911.
Brière CA. 189 — Cat. impr. 271 — S.A.I. 1394 —
C.P.t.l. p. 271.

F.R. 2005
THE WATER-LILY POND. HARNOMY IN PINK.
T. H. 0.895; W. 1.00.
S.D.b.g.: Monet, 1900.
Camondo bequest, 1911.
Brière CA. 190 — Cat. impr. 272 — S.A.I. 1395 —
C.P.t.l. p. 271.

VETHEUIL SUNSET
T.H. 0.89; W. 0.92.
S.D.b.g.: Claude Monet, 1901.
Camondo bequest, 1911.
Brière CA. 191 — Cat. impr. 273 — S.A.I. 1396 —
C.P.t.l. p. 271.

F.R. 2007
LONDON THE PARLIAMENT. SUN PIERCING
THROUGH FOG
T. H. 0.81; W. 0.92.
S.D.b.g.: Claude Monet, 1904.
Camondo bequest, 1911.
Brière CA. 192 — Cat. impr. 275 — S.A.I. 1398 —
C.P.t.l. p. 271.

F.R. 2623
SELF-PORTRAIT
T. H. 0.70; W. 0.55.
Painted in 1917.
Presented by Georges Clemenceau, 1927.
Cat. impr. 276 — S.A.I. 1399 — C.P.t.l. p. 272.

INV. 20100 to 20107
WATER-LILIES. STUDY OF WATER
Decoration comprising an ensemble of eight
compositions painted at Giverny between 1914
and 1922, completed and placed in the *Orangery
of Les Tuileries* in the order indicated by the artist
before his death in 1926. Inaugurated in 1927.
Claude Monet donation, 1922.
C.P.t.l. p. 269.

(INV. 20101)
MORNING
T. H. 1.97; W. 12.11.
First Water-lilies Room, on the right.
S.A.I. 1401.

(INV. 20102)
GREEN REFLECTIONS
T. H. 1.97; W. 8.47.
First Water-lilies Room, at the back.
S.A.I. 1402.

(INV. 20100)
CLOUDS
T. H. 1.97; W. 12.71.
First Water-lilies Room, on the left.
S.A.I. 1400.

(INV. 20103)
SUNSET
T. H. 1.97; W. 5.94.
First Water-lilies Room, between the two doors.
S.A.I. 1403.

(INV. 20106)
MORNING
T. H. 1.97; W. 12.77.
Second Water-lilies Room, on the right.
S.A.I. 1406.

(INV. 20104)
THE TWO WILLOW-TREES
T. H. 1.97; W. 16.90.
Second Water-lilies Room, at the back.
S.A.I. 1405.

(INV. 20105)
MORNING
T. H. 1.97; W. 12.77.
Second Water-lilies Room, on the left.
S.A.I. 1405.

(INV. 20107).
REFLECTIONS OF TREES
T. H. 1.97; W. 8.48.
Second Water-lilies Room, between the two doors.

MOREAU-NÉLATON Etienne
Paris, 1859-1927.

F.R. 3791
THE SQUARE AT FÈRE-EN-TARDENOIS
T. H. 0.38; W. 0.46.
S.D.b.g.: Etienne Moreau-Nélaton, 86, Fère.
Bequeathed by M. and Mme Raymond Koechlin
1931.
Cat. impr. 283 — S.A.I. 1425 — C.P.t.L. p. 279.

MORISOT Berthe
Bourges, 1841 - Paris, 1895.

F.R. 2849
THE CRADLE
Mme Pontillon, née Edma Morisot, the artist's
sister, with her daughter Blanche.
T. H. 0.56; W. 0.46.
Painted in 1872.
(Bataille et Wildenstein 25).
Acquired in 1930.
Cat. impr. 286 — S.A.I. 1428 — C.P.t.l. p. 280.

F.R. 1681
THE BUTTERFLY CATCHERS
Mme Pontillon, née Edma Morisot,
tje artist's sister, with her daughters Jeanne
and Blanche.
S.b.d.: Berthe Morisot.
(Bataille et Wildenstein 36).
Etienne Moreau-Nélaton donation, 1906.
Brière M. 84 — Cat. impr. 285 — S.A.I. 1427 —
C.P.t.l. p. 280.

F.R. 1937-45
IN THE CORNFIELD
T. H. 0.465; W. 0.690.
S.b.g.: Berthe Morisot.
Painted in 1875.
(Bataille et Wildenstein 46).
Antonin Personnaz bequest, 1937.
Cat. impr. 287 — S.A.I. 1429 — C.P.t.l. p. 280.

F.R. 1937-44
YOUNG WOMAN POWDERING HER FACE
T. H. 0.46; W. 0.39.
S.b.g.: Berthe Morisot.
Painted in 1877.
(Bataille et Wildenstein 72).
Antonin Personnaz bequest, 1937.
Cat. impr. 288 — S.A.I. 1431 — C.P.t.l. p. 280.

F.R. 843
YOUNG WOMAN DRESSED FOR THE BALL
T. H. 0.71; W. 0.54.
S.b.g.: Berthe Morisot.
Painted in 1879.
(Bataille et Wildenstein 72).
Acquired in 1894.
Cat. impr. 289 — S.A.I. 1430 — C.P.t.l. p. 279.

F.R. 1969-22
LOUISE RIESENER (born 1860),
daughter of the painter Léon Riesener, later
Mme Léouzan-le-Duc.
T. H. 0.735; W. 0.930.
S.h.g.: B. Morisot.
Painted in 1888.
(Bataille et Wildenstein 222).
Bequeathed by Mme Raymond Escholier,

née Claude Léouzan-le-Duc, daughter of the sitter,
1969.

F.R. 1945-13
THE CHILDREN OF GABRIEL THOMAS,
first cousin to the artist and art-collector.
T. H. 1.000; W. 0.812.
S.b. towards the right: B. Morisot.
Painted in 1894.
(Bataille et Wildenstein 367).
Presented by the children of Gabriel Thomas, in
memory of their parents, 1945.
C.P.t.l. p. 280.

F.R. 2268
HORTENSIA, also known as THE TWO SISTERS
T. H. 0.735; W. 0.605.
Painted in 1894.
(Bataille et Wildenstein 371).
Presented by Ernest Rouart et Mme, née Manet,
the artist's daughter, 1920.
Cat. impr. 290 — S.A.I. 1432 — C.P.t.l. p. 280.

MURER Eugène,
also known as MEUNIER Auguste
Moulins, 1845 - Auvers-sur-Oise, 1906.

F.R. 1955-8
THE RIVER OISE AT L'ISLE-ADAM
T. H. 0.46; W. 0.65.
S.b.g. : Murer.
Painted ap. 1903.
Presented by Paul Gachet, 1955.
Cat. impr. 291 — S.A.I. 1446 — C.P.t.l. p. 282.

OLLER y CESTERO Francisco
Puerto-Rico, 1833 — Santurce (Porto-Rico), 1917.

F.R. 1953-19
BANKS OF THE SEINE
C. H. 0.25; W. 0.34.
S.D.b.g.: Oller 1875.
Presented by Dr. Martinez, 1953.
Cat. impr. 293 — S.A.I. 1450.

F.R. 1951-41
THE STUDENT
T. H. 0.64; W. 0.55.
S.b.d.: F. Oller.
Presented by Paul Gachet, 1951.
Cat. impr. 294 — S.A.I. 1451.

OSBERT Alphonse
Paris, 1857-1939

R.F. 1957-6
PORTRAIT OF ANTONIN PERSONNAZ
B. H. 0.30; W. 0.24.
Ap. 1885.
Acquired in 1957.
Cat. impr. 295 — S.A.I. 1452 — C.P.t.l. p. 286.

PISSARRO Camille
Saint-Thomas (Danish West Indies), 1830 - Paris,
1903.

F.R. 1943-8
VIEW FROM MONTMORENCY

B. H. 0.216; W. 0.273.
S.b.g.: Camille Pizarro.
Painted ap. 1859.
Presented by Baron d'Albenas with reservation
of usufruct, 1943 ; entered 1976.

F.R. 1951-38
THE FERRY-BOAT AT LA VARENNE-SAINT-HILAIRE
T. H. 0.27; W. 0.41.
S.D.b.d.: C. Pierre Pissarro, 64.
(Pissarro et Venturi 36).
Presented by Paul Gachet, 1951.
Cat impr. 296 — S.A.I. 1465 — C.P.t.l. p. 298.

F.R. 1937-50
THE LOUVECIENNES ROAD
T. H. 0.465; W. 0.550.
S.D.b.d.: C. Pissarro, 1870.
(Pissarro et Venturi 79).
Antonin Personnaz bequest, 1937).
Cat. impr. 298 — S.A.I. 1468 — C.P.t.l. p. 297.

F.R. 1937-58
COUNTRY COTTAGE. THE PINK HOUSE
T. H. 0.460; W. 0.555.
S.D.b.g.: C. Pissarro, 1870.
(Pissarro et Venturi 82).
Antonin Personnaz bequest, 1937.
Cat. impr. 300 — S.A.I. 1466 — C.P.t.l. p. 298.

F.R. 1682
THE COACH AT LOUVECIENNES
T. H. 0.255; W. 0.357.
S.D.b.g.: C. Pissarro, 1870.
(Pissarro et Venturi 80).
Etienne Moreau-Nélaton donation, 1906.
Brière M. 85 — Cat. impr. 299 — S.A.I. 1467 —
C.P.t.l. p. 295.

F.R. 1937-54
WINTER LANDSCAPE AT LOUVECIENNES
T. H. 0.37; W. 0.46.
S.b.g.: C. Pissarro.
Painted ap. 1870.
(Pissarro et Venturi 81).
Antonin Personnaz bequest, 1937.
Cat. impr. 301 — S.A.I. 1469 — C.P.t.l. p. 298.

F.R. 1937-56
HILLSIDES AT LE VÉSINET
T. H. 0.435; W. 0.655.
S.D.b.d.: C. Pissarro, 1871.
(Pissarro et Venturi 117).
Antonin Personnaz bequest, 1937.
Cat. impr. 302 — S.A.I. 1470 — C.P.t.l. p. 298.

F.R. 2732
THE WASH-HOUSE AT PONTOISE
T. H. 0.465; W. 0.560.
S.D.b.g.: C. Pissarro, 1872.
(Pissarro et Venturi 175).
Gustave Caillebotte bequest, 1894; entered 1896.
Cat. impr. 305 — S.A.I. 1475 — C.P.t.l. p. 296.

F.R. 1951-37
THE LOUVECIENNES ROAD
T. H. 0.600, W. 0.735.
S.D.b.g.: C. Pissarro, 1872.
(Pissarro et Venturi 138).
Presented by Paul Gachet, 1951.
Cat. impr. 304 — S.A.I. 1472 — C.P.t.l. p. 298.

F.R. 1683
PONTOISE
T. H. 0.405; W. 0.545.
S.D.b.d.: C. Pissarro, 1872.
(Pissarro et Venturi 172).
Etienne Moreau-Nélaton donation, 1906.
Brière M. 86 — Cat. impr. 306 — S.A.I. 1473 —
C.P.t.l. p. 295.

F.R. 1954-18
CHESTNUT-TREES AT LOUVECIENNES
T. H. 0.41; W. 0.54.
S.b.d. : C. Pissarro.
Painted ap. 1872.
(Pissarro et Venturi 146).
Presented by Paul Gachet, 1954.
Cat. impr. 297 — S.A.I. 1471 — C.P.t.l. p. 299.

F.R. 2436
ENTRY TO THE VILLAGE OF VOISINS
T. H. 0.460; W. 0.555.
S.D.b.d.: C. Pissarro, 1872.
(Pissarro et Venturi 141).
Donated by Ernest May, with reservation of
usufruct, 1923; entered the Louvre Museum 1926.
Cat. impr. 303 — S.A.I. 1474 — C.P.t.l. p. 296.

F.R. 2837
SELF-PORTRAIT
T.H. 0.560; W. 0.467.
S.D.b.g.: C. Pissarro, 1873.
(Pissarro et Venturi 200).
Donated by Paul-Emile Pissarro, the artist's son,
with reservation of usufruct, 1930; entered the
Louvre Museum 1947.
Cat. impr. 307 — S.A.I. 1476 — C.P.t.l. p. 296.

F.R. 1972-27
HOAR-FROST
T. H. 0.65; W. 0.93.
S.D.b.g.: C. Pissarro, 1873.
(Pissarro et Venturi 203).
Eduardo Mollard bequest, 1972.

F.R. 1973-19
THE ENNERY ROAD NEAR PONTOISE
T. H. 0.55; W. 0.92.
S.D.b.g.: C. Pissarro, 1874.
(Pissarro et Venturi 254).
M. and R. Kaganovitch donation, 1973.

F.R. 1972-28
LANDSCAPE AT PONTOISE
T. H. 0.515; W. 0.81.
S.b.d.: C. Pissarro.
Painted ap. 1875.
(Pissarro et Venturi 309).
Edouard Mollard bequest, 1972.

F.R. 3756
HARVEST AT MONTFOUCAULT
T. H. 0.650; W. 0.925.
S.D.b.g.: C. Pissarro, 1876.
(Pissarro et Venturi 364).
Gustave Caillebotte bequest, 1894; entered 1896.
Cat. impr. 308 — S.A.I. 1477 — C.P.t.l. p. 297.

F.R. 1951-11
THE COACH, THE ENNERY ROAD AT THE
HERMITAGE, PONTOISE
T. H. 0.465; W. 0.550.
S.D.b.g.: C. Pissarro, 77.

(Pissarro et Venturi 411).
Presented by Dr. And Mme Albert Charpentier,
1951.
Cat. impr. 309 — S.A.I. 1478 — C.P.t.l. p. 298.

F.R. 2735
RED ROOFS, A CORNER OF THE VILLAGE.
A STUDY IN WINTER.
T. H. 0.545; W. 0.656.
S.D.b.d.: C. Pissarro 1877.
(Pissarro et Venturi 384).
Gustave Caillebotte bequest, 1894; entered 1896.
Cat. impr. 312 — S.A.I. 1481 — S.P.t.l. p. 296.

F.R. 2731
UNDERGROWTH, IN SUMMER
T. H. 0.810; W. 0.657.
S.D.b.d.: C. Pissarro, 1877.
(Pissarro et Venturi 416).
Gustave Caillebotte bequest, 1894; entered 1896.
Cat. impr. 310 — S.A.I. 479 — C.P.t.l. p. 296.

F.R. 2733
KITCHEN-GARDEN AND TREES IN BLOSSOM
SPRING. PONTOISE
T. H. 0.655; W. 0.810.
S.D.b.g.: C. Pissarro, 1877.
(Pissarro et Venturi 387).
Gustave Caillebotte bequest, 1894; entered 1896.
Cat. impr. 311 — S.A.I. 1480 — C.P.t.l. p. 296.

F.R. 1973-20
GARDEN PLOT AT L'HERMITAGE
T. H. 0.55; W. 0.46.
S.D.b.d.: C. Pissarro 1877.
(Pissarro et Venturi 396).
Max and Rosy Kaganovitch donation, 1973.

F.R. 1937-57
BANKS OF THE RIVER OISE, NEAR PONTOISE,
IN CLOUDY WEATHER
T. H. 0.545; W. 0.655.
S.D.b.d.: Pissarro, 1878.
(Pissarro et Venturi 434).
Antonin Personnaz bequest, 1937.
Cat. impr. 313 — S.A.I. 1482 — C.P.t.l. p. 298.

F.R. 2736
UPHILL ROAD ACROSS FIELDS,
NEAR LES GRIOTTES, PONTOISE
T. H. 0.540; W. 0.655.
S.D.b.g.: C. Pissarro, 79.
(Pissarro et Venturi 493).
Gustave Caillebotte bequest, 1894; entered 1896.
Cat. impr. 314 — S.A.I. 1483 — C.P.t.l. p. 296.

F.R. 1937-48
KITCHEN-GARDEN AT L'HERMITAGE, PONTOISE
T. H. 0.550; W. 0.655.
S.D.n.d.: C. Pissarro, 79.
(Pissarro et Venturi 496).
Antonin Personnaz bequest, 1937.
Cat. impr. 315 — S.A.I. 1484 — C.P.t.l. p. 297.

F.R. 1937-51
LANDSCAPE AT CHAPONVAL
T.H. 0.545; W. 0.650.
S.D.b.d.: C. Pissarro, 80.
(Pissarro et Venturi 509).
Antonin Personnaz bequest, 1937.
Cat. impr. 316 — S.A.I. 1486 — C.P.t.l. p. 297.

F.R. 2734
THE WHEELBARROW. ORCHARD
T. H. 0.54; W. 0.65.
Ap. 1881.
(Pissarro et Venturi 537).
Gustave Caillebotte bequest, 1894; entered 1896.
Cat. impr. 317 — S.A.I. 1485 — C.P.t.l. p. 296.

F.R. 2013
GIRL WITH A STICK. SEATED PEASANT
T. H. 0.810; W. 0.647.
S.D.b.d.: C. Pissarro, 1881.
(Pissarro et Venturi 540).
Camondo bequest, 1911.
Brière CA. 193 — Cat. impr. 318 — S.A.I. 1487 —
C.P.t.l. p. 295.

F.R. 1937-47
WOMAN IN A CLOSE. SPRING SUNSHINE,
IN THE FIELD AT ERAGNY
T. H. 0.545; W. 0.650.
S.D.b.d.: C. Pissarro, 1887.
(Pissarro et Venturi 709).
Antonin Personnaz bequest, 1937.
Cat. impr. 319 — S.A.I. 1488 — C.P.t.l. p. 297.

F.R. 1972-29
WOMAN HANGING OUT WASHING
T.H. 0.41; W. 0.325.
S.D.b.g.: C. Pissarro, 1887.
(Pissarro et Venturi 717).
Eduardo Mollard bequest, 1972.

F.R. 1972-30
WOMAN WITH A GREEN KERCHIEF
T. H. 0.655; W. 0.545.
S.D.h.g.: C. Pissarro, 1893.
(Pissarro et Venturi 854).
Eduardo Mollard bequest, 1972.

F.R. 2014
SNOW EFFECT AT ERAGNY (OISE)
T. H. 0.735; W. 0.925.
S.D.b.d.: C. Pissarro, 94.
(Pissarro et Venturi 867).
Camondo bequest, 1911.
Brière CA. 194 — Cat. impr. 320 — S.A.I. 1490 —
C.P.t.l. p. 295.

F.R. 1937-53
THE CHURCH AT KNOKKE (Belgium)
T. H. 0.545; W. 0.655.
S.D.b.g.: C. Pissarro, 94.
(Pissarro et Venturi 890).
Antonin Personnaz bequest, 1937.
Cat. impr. 321 — S.A.I. 1489 — C.P.t.l. p. 297.

F.R. 1937-59
LANDSCAPE AT ERAGNY.
THE CHURCH AND FARM AT ERAGNY
T. H. 0.600; W. 0.734.
S.D.b.d.: C. Pissarro, 95.
(Pissarro et Venturi 929).
Antonin Personnaz bequest, 1937.
Cat. impr. 322 — S.A.I. 1491 — C.P.t.l. p. 298.

F.R. 1972-31
THE HARBOUR AT ROUEN. SAINT-SEVER
T.H. 0.655; W. 0.92.
S.D.b.g.: C. Pissarro, 1896.
(Pissaro et Venturi 957).
Eduardo Mollard bequest, 1972.

F.R. 1937-46
WOMAN IN AN ORCHARD. AUTUMN MORNING.
GARDEN IN ERAGNY
T. H. 0.545; W. 0.650.
S.D.b.g.: C. Pissarro, 97.
(Pissarro et Venturi 1016).
Antonin Personnaz bequest, 1937.
Cat. impr. 323 — S.A.I. 1492 — C.P.t.l. p. 297.

F.R. 1937-52
THE WASH-HOUSE AT BAZINCOURT
T. H. 0.655; W. 0.810.
S.D.b.d.: C. Pissarro, 1900.
(Pissarro et Venturi 1141).
Antonin Personnaz bequest, 1937.
Cat. impr. 324 — S.A.I. 1493 — C.P.t.l. p. 297).

M.N.R. 222
CHURCH OF SAINT-JACQUES AT DIEPPE
T. H. 0.545; W. 0.655.
S.D.b.g.: C. Pissarro, 1901.
Attributed to the Louvre Museum by the Private
Properties Office, 1950.
Cat. impr. 325 — S.A.I. 1494 — C.P.t.l. p. 299.

F.R. 1937-55
DIEPPE. THE DUQUESNE DOCK, LOW TIDE,
MORNING SUN.
T. H. 0.545; W. 0.650.
S.D.b.d.: C. Pissarro, 1902.
(Pissarro et Venturi 1253).
Antonin Personnaz bequest, 1937.
Cat. impr. 326 — S.A.I. 1496 — C.P.t.l. p. 298.

F.R. 1937-49
MORET, THE LOING CANAL
T. H. 0.650; W. 0.815.
S.D.b.g.: C. Pissarro, 1902.
(Pissarro et Venturi 1237).
Antonin Personnaz bequest, 1937.
Cat. impr. 327 — S.A.I. 1496 — C.P.t.l. p. 297.

F.R. 1972-32
THE RIVER SEINE AND THE LOUVRE
T. H. 0.46; W. 0.55.
S.D.b.g.: C. Pissarro, 1903.
(Pissarro et Venturi 1278).
Eduardo Mollard bequest, 1972.

REDON Odilon

Bordeaux, 1840 - Paris, 1916.

F.R. 2703
MADAME ODILON REDON, née Camille Falte
(1853-1923).
T. H. 0.455; W. 0.375.
S.D.b.g.: 1882, Odilon Redon.
Presented by Mme J. Groekoop de Jong, 1926.
Cat. impr. 332 — S.A.U. 1554 — C.P.t.l. p. 315.

F.R. 1941-23
VASE OF FLOWERS. THE RED POPPY
T. H. 0.27; W. 0.19.
S.b.g.: Odilon Redon.
Bequeathed by Paul Jamot, 1941.
Cat. impr. 334 — S.A.I. 1556 — C.P.t.l. p. 315.

F.R. 2791
CLOSED EYES
T. on carton. H. 0.44; W. 0.36.
S.D.b.g.: Odilon Redon, 1890.
Acquired in 1904.

Cat. impr. 333 — S.A.I. 1555. — C.P.t.l. p. 315.

INV. 20612
FLOWERS
T. H. 0.46; W. 0.38.
S.b.d.: Odilon Redon.
Painted before 1900.
Philippon bequest, 1939.

F.R. 1950-31
PAUL GAUGUIN (1848-1903) painter
T. H. 0.660; W. 0.545.
S.b.d.: Odilon Redon.
Painted after Gauguin's death, between 1903
and 1905.
Acquired in 1950.
Cat. impr. 335 — S.A.I. 1557 — C.P.t.l. p. 315.

RENOIR Pierre-Auguste

Limoges, 1841 - Cagnes-sur-Mer (Var), 1919.

F.R. 1952-3
WILLIAM SISLEY (†1871), father of Sisley
the painter
T. H. 0.815; W. 0.655.
S.D. mi-h.g.: A. Renoir, 1864.
1865 Salon.
(Daulte 11).
Acquired in 1952.
Cat. impr. 337 — S.A.I. 1573 — C.P.t.l. p. 322.

F.R. 2448
FRÉDÉRIC BAZILLE (1841-1870) painter
T. H. 1.050; W. 0.735.
S.D.b.d.: A. Renoir, 67.
(Daulte 28).
Bequeathed by Marc Bazille, brother of the sitter,
1924.
Cat. impr. 338 — S.A.I. 1574 — C.P.t.l. p. 318.

F.R. 3667
LIGHTERS ON THE SEINE
T. H. 0.47; W. 0.64.
S.b.d.: Renoir.
Painted in 1869.
Bequeathed by M. and Mme Raymond Koechlin,
1931.
Cat. impr. 339 — S.A.I. 1576 — C.P.t.l. p. 372.

F.R. 2741
MADAME THÉODORE CHARPENTIER,
née Marie-Pauline Le Grand (1802-1875).
Mother-in-law of Charles-le-Cœur, architect
and friend of Renoir.
T. H. 0.46; W. 0.39.
S.d. above the shoulder: A. Renoir.
Painted ap. 1869.
(Daulte 53).
Presented by François Le Cœur, grandson of
the sitter and of Madame, née Charpentier, 1924.
Cat. impr. 340 — S.A.I. 1575 — C.P.t.l. p. 319.

F.R. 2443
SEMI-NUDE WOMAN RECLINING: THE ROSE
T. H. 0.295; W. 0.250.
S.b.d.: Renoir.
Painted ap. 1872.
(Daulte 82).
Ernest May donation, with reservation of usufruct,
1923; entered the Louvre Museum 1926.
Cat. impr. 341 — S.A.I. 1577 — C.P.t.l. p. 318.

F.R. 1965-11
MADAME DARRAS, wife of Captain Darras,
a friend of the Le Cœur family.
T. H. 0.475; W. 0.390.
S.b.g.: A. Renoir.
Study for "The Amazon," painted in 1873
(Kunsthalle, Hamburg).
(Daulte 93).
Presented by Baroness Eva Gebhard-Gourgaud,
1965.
C.P.t.l. p. 322.

F.R. 1951-14
THE SEINE AT ARGENTEUIL
T. H. 0.465; W. 0.650.
S.b.d.: Renoir.
Painted ap. 1873.
Presented by Dr. and Mme Albert Charpentier,
1951.
Cat impr. 342 — S.A.I. 1578 — C.P.t.l. p. 321.

F.R. 2792
PORTRAIT OF A WOMAN, also known as
MME G. HARTMANN
T. H. 0.83; W. 1.23.
S.D.b.g.: A. Renoir, 74
(Daulte 112).
Presented by General Bourjat, 1902.
Cat. impr. 343 — S.A.I. 1579 — C.P.t.l. p. 319.

F.R. 1961-22
Charles Le Cœur (1830-1906), architect, brother
of the painter Jules Le Cœur, a friend of Renoir.
T. H. 0.42; W. 0.29.
S.b.g.: A. Renoir.
Painted in 1874.
(Daulte 99).
Eduardo Mollard donation, 1961.
C.P.t.l. p. 322.

F.R. 3757
WOMAN READING
T. H. 0.465; W. 0.385.
S. mi-h.g.: Renoir.
Painted in 1874.
(Daulte 106).
Gustave Caillebotte bequest, 1894; entered 1896.
Cat. impr. 348 — S.A.I. 1582 — C.P.t.l. p. 320.

F.R. 3666
CLAUDE MONET (1840-1926), painter
T. H. 0.850; W. 0.605.
S.D.b.d.: Renoir, 75.
(Daulte 132)
Bequeathed by M. and Mme Raymond Koechlin,
1931.
Cat. impr. 344 — S.A.I. 1580 — C.P.t.l. p. 320.

F.R. 3668
YOUNG WOMAN WITH A HAT-VEIL
T. H. 0.61; W. 0.51.
S.b.d.: Renoir (signature smudged).
Painted ap. 1875.
(Daulte 151).
Bequeathed by M. and Mme Raymond Koechlin,
1931.
Cat. impr. 354 — S.A.I. 1583 — C.P.t.l. p. 320.

F.R. 1953-3
YOUNG WOMAN SITTING IN A GARDEN
B. H. 0.100; W. 0.085.
S.d.b.: Renoir.

Painted ap. 1875.
(Daulte 140).
Bequeathed by Carle Dreyfus, 1953.
Cat. impr. 347 — S.A.I. 1584 — C.P.t.I. p. 322.

F.R. 2737
BY THE SEINE AT CHAMPROSAY
T. H. 0.55; W. 0.66.
S.b.d.: Renoir.
Painted in 1876.
Gustave Caillebotte bequest, 1894; entered 1896.
Cat. impr. 349 — S.A.I. 1585 — C.P.t.I. p. 319.

M.N.R. 201
MADAME ALPHONSE DAUDET, née Julie Allard
(1844-1940), wife of the writer
T. H. 0.46; W. 0
S.D.b.d.: Renoir, 76.
(Daulte 163).
Attributed to the Louvre Museum by the Private
Properties Office, 1951.
Cat. impr. 350 — S.A.I. 1586 — C.P.t.I. p. 322.

F.R. 2738
THE SWING
T. H. 0.92; W. 0.73.
S.D.b.d. : Renoir, 76.
Daulte 202).
Gustave Caillebotte bequest, 1894; entered 1896.

F.R. 2739
THE MOULIN DE LA GALETTE, Montmartre
T. H. 1.31; W. 1.75.
S.D.b.d.: Renoir, 76.
(Daulte 209).
Gustave Caillebotte bequest, 1894; entered 1896.
Cat. impr. 351 — S.A.I. 1588 — C.P.t.I. 319.

F.R. 2740
TORSO OF A WOMAN, IN SUNLIGHT
T. H. 0.810; W. 0.648.
S.b.d.: Renoir.
Painted ap. 1876.
(Daulte 201).
Gustave Caillebotte bequest, 1894; entered 1896.
Cat. impr. 345 — S.A.I. 1581 — C.P.t.I. p. 319.

F.R. 2581
PATH THROUGH TALL GRASS
T. H. 0.60; W. 0.74.
S.b.g. : Renoir.
Painted ap. 1876-77.
Presented by Charles Comiot through the Society
of Friend of the Louvre Museum, 1926.
Cat. impr. 346; S.A.I. 1589 — C.P.t.I. p. 319.

F.R. 2244
MADAME GEORGES CHARPENTIER,
née Marguerite Lemonnier, wife of the publisher.
T. H. 0.463; W. 0.380.
S.h.d.;: Renoir.
Painted ap. 1876-77.
(Daulte 226).
Presented by the Society of Friends of
the Luxembourg Museum, 1919.
Cat. impr. 353 — S.A.I. 1590 — C.P.t.I. p. 318.

F.R. 1951-39
PORTRAIT OF MARGOT.
T. H. 0.465; W. 0.380.
S.h. towards the left: Renoir.
Painted 1878.
(Daulte 276).

Presented by Paul Gachet, 1951.
Cat. impr. 355 — S.A.I. 1591 — C.P.t.I. p. 322.

F.R. 1878-41
MADAME PAUL BÉRARD,
née Marguerite Girod (1844-1901)
T.H. 0.495; W. 0.40.
S.D.h.d.: Renoir, 79.
(Daulte 283).
In lieu of payment of death duties, 1978.

F.R. 1952-33
SELF-PORTRAIT
T. H. 0.19; W. 0.14.
S.b.d.: Renoir.
Painted 1879.
(Daulte 293).
Presented by M. D. Guérin with reservation
of usufruct, 1952; usufruct abandoned in 1974.

F.R. 1937-9
ALFONSINE FOURNAISE (1845-1937),
daughter of a restaurant-keeper in the île de
Chatou (Yvelines), between Chatou and Rueil,
also known as La Grenouillère.
T. H. 0.735; W. 0.930.
S.D.b.d. : Renoir, 79.
(Daulte 301).
Presented by D. David-Weil, 1937.
Cat. impr. 356 — S.A.I. 1592 — C.P.t.I. p. 320.

F.R. 1961-21
PORTRAIT OF A WOMAN WITH A WHITE
SHIRT-FRILL.
T. H. 0.463; W. 0.380.
S.D.h.d.: Renoir, 80.
(Daulte 352).
Edouardo Mollard donation, 1961.
C.P.t.I. p. 322.

F.R. 1943-62
ALGERIAN LANDSCAPE. THE WILD-WOMAN-
RAVINE (suburb of Algiers)
T. H. 0.655; W. 0.810.
S.b.g.: Renoir.
Painted 1881.
Acquired in 1943.
Cat. impr. 359 — S.A.I. 1595 — C.P.t.I. p. 321.

F.R. 1957-8
ARAB FÊTE AT ALGIERS. THE CASBAH
T. H. 0.735; W. 0.920.
S.D.b.d.: Renoir, 81.
Presented by the Biddle Foundation, 1957,
in memory of Mrs. Margaret Biddle.
Cat. impr. 358 — S.A.I. 1594 — C.P.t.I. p. 322.

F.R. 1959-1
BANANA FIELDS
T. H. 0.515; W. 0.635.
S.D.b.d.: Renoir, 81.
Acquired in 1959.
Cat. impr. 359 bis — S.A.I. 1596 — C.P.t.I. p. 322.

F.R. 3758
THE RAILWAY BRIDGE AT CHATOU (Yvelines)
T. H. 0.540; W. 0.657.
S.D.b.d.: Renoir, 81 (signature added subsequently
by Renoir).
Gustave Caillebotte bequest, 1894; entered 1896.
Cat. impr. 357 — S.A.I. 1593 — C.P.t.I. p. 320.

F.R. 1947-11
RICHARD WAGNER (1813-1883) composer
T. H. 0.53; W. 0.46.
S.h.d.: Renoir. D.h.d.: 15 January 82.
(Daulte 394).
Presented by Alfred Cortot with reservation of
usufruct in memory of his first wife, 1947;
entered the Louvre Museum 1963.
C.P.t.I. p. 321.

F.R. 1978-13
DANCE IN THE CITY
T. H. 1.80; W. 0.90.
S.D.b.d.: Renoir, 83.
(Daulte 440).
Acquired in lieu of payment of death-duties, 1978.

F.R. 1973-22
SEASCAPE, GUERNSEY
T. H. 0.46; W. 0.56.
S.b.g.: Renoir.
Painted in 1883.
Donation M. and R. Kaganovitch, 1973.

F.R. 1973-21
GLADIOLI
T. H. 0.75; W. 0.545.
S.b.g. and dedicated to Dr. Latty: A souvenir
of friendship.
Renoir.
Painted ap. 1885;
M. and R. Kaganovitch donation.

F.R. 1974-5
STILL-LIFE
T. H. 0.465; W. 0.555.
S.b.d.: Renoir.
Retouched painting (A. Vollard, Tableau, pastels
et dessins de P.-A. Renoir, 2 vol. Paris, 1918.
V. II, plate repr. p. 45) Attributed by the Ministry
of Economy and Finance, 1974.

M.N.R. 579
WOMAN AT A WELL
B. H. 0.35; W. 0.27.
S.b.g.: A.R.
Uncompleted work.
(A Vollard, Tableaux, pastels et dessins de P.-A.
Renoir, 2 vol. Paris, 1918. V. II, repr. p. 29;
Daulte 501, as painted ap. 1886).
Attributed to the Louvre Museum by the Private
Properties Office, 1951.

F.R. 1937-61
BUST OF A YOUNG WOMAN NUDE
T. H. 0.35; W. 0.27.
S.h.d.: Renoir.
Painted ap. 1886.
(Daulte 508).
Antonin Personnaz bequest, 1937.
Cat. impr. 362 — S.AI. 1599 — C.P.t.I. p. 320.

F.R. 1941-26
MOSS-ROSES
T. H. 0.355; W. 0.270.
S.b.d.: Renoir.
Painted ap. 1890.
Bequeathed by Paul Jamot, 1941.
Cat. impr. 361 — S.A.I. 1598 — C.P.t.I. p. 320.

M.N.R. 580
ROSES IN A VASE

T. H. 0.295; W. 0.330.
S.b.d.: Renoir.
Painted ap. 1890.
Attributed to the Louvre Museum by the Private
Properties Office, 1951.
Cat. impr. 363 — S.A.I. 1601 — C.P.t.l. p. 323.

F.R. 755
GIRLS AT THE PIANO
T. H. 1.16; W. 0.90.
S.b.d.: Renoir.
Painted in 1892; commissioned by the State.
Acquired in 1892.
Cat. impr. 364 — S.A.I. 1600 — C.P.t.l. p. 318.

F.R. 1937-60
READER IN GREEN
T. H. 0.265; W. 0.210.
S.b.d.: Renoir.
Painted ap. 1894.
Antonin Personnaz bequest, 1937.
Cat. impr. 365 — S.A.I. 1602 — C.P.t.l. p. 320.

F.R. 1961-3
NUDE. Uncompleted study.
T. H. 0.353; W. 0.225.
S.h.d.: Renoir.
Painted ap. 1895.
Bequeathed by M. and Mme Frédéric Lung, 1961.
C.P.t.l. p. 322.

F.R. 1951-29
MADAME GASTON BERNHEIM DE VILLERS,
née Suzanne Adler (1883-1961).
T. H. 0.93; W. 0.73.
S.D.b.d.: Renoir, 1901.
Presented by M. and Mme Gaston Bernheim
de Villers, 1951.
Cat. impr. 368 — S.A.I. 1604 — C.P.t.l. p. 321.

M.N.R. 838
ODE TO FLOWERS (after Anacreon).
T. H. 0.46; W. 0.36.
S.b.g.: Renoir.
Painted ap. 1903-1909.
Attributed to the Louvre Museum by the Private
Properties Office, 1951.
Cat. impr. 370 — S.A.I. 1605 — C.P.t.l. p. 323.

F.R. 2016
THE TOILET. WOMAN COMBING HER HAIR
T. H. 0.550; W. 0.465.
S.h.g.: Renoir.
Painted ap. 1907-08.
Camondo bequest, 1911.
Brière C.A. 198 — Cat. impr. 375 — S.A.I. 1610.
C.P.t.l. p. 318

F.R. 2017
LITTLE GIRL WITH A STRAW HAT
T. H. 0.46; W. 0.35.
S.h.d.: Renoir.
Painted ap. 1908.
Camondo bequest, 1911.
Brière CA. 196 — Cat. impr. 369 — S.A.I. 1606.
C.P.t.l. p. 318.

F.R. 1951-16
RECLINING NUDE, BACK VIEW
T. H. 0.41; W. 0.52.
S.b.g.: Renoir.
Painted ap. 1909.

Presented by Dr. and Mme Albert Charpentier, 1951.
Cat. impr. 372 — S.A.I. 1608 — C.P.t.l. p. 321.

R.F. 2018
GIRL SEATED, Hélène Bellon, later Mme Garrache,
then Mme Forestieri (1890-1950).
T. H. 0.655; W. 0.545.
S.b.d.: Renoir.
Painted 1909.
Camondo bequest, 1911.
Brière C.A. 197 — Cat. impr. 271 — S.A.I. 1607.
C.P.t.l. p. 318.

F.R. 1951-28
MONSIEUR AND MADAME BERNHEIM DE VILLERS.
Gaston Bernheim de Villers (1870-1953) director
of an art gallery in Paris, and his wife, née Suzanne
Adler (1883-1961).
T. H. 0.810; W. 0.655.
S.D.h.d.: Renoir, 10.
Presented by M. and Mme Bernheim de Villers, 1951.
Cat. impr. 374 — S.A.I. 1611 — C.P.t.l. p. 321.

F.R. 1951-30
GENEVIÈVE BERNHEIM DE VILLERS (1907-1936),
daughter of M. and Mme Bernheim de Villers.
T. H. 0.53; W. 0.44.
S.D.h.d.: Renoir, 10.
Presented by M. and Mme Bernheim de Villers, 1951.
Cat. impr. 373 — S.A.I. 1609 — C.P.t.l. p. 321.

F.R. 2491
GABRIELLE WITH A ROSE
T. H. 0.555; W. 0.470.
S.D.h.d.: Renoir, 1911. On the back an
inscription on the frame: Cagnes, 1911.
Presented by Philippe Gangnat, 1925.
Cat. impr. 376 — S.A.I. 1613 — C.P.t.l. p. 319.

F.R. 2796
YOUNG WOMAN WITH ROSE   WOMAN IN BLUE
Mme Colonna Romano, actress at the Comédie-
Française, born 1883.
T. H. 0.655; W. 0.545.
Painted 1913.
Presented by the artist, 1918.
Cat. impr. 377 — S.A.I. 1614 — C.P.t.l. p. 320.

M.N.R. 199
GATHERING IN A GARDEN
T. H. 0.55; W. 0.65.
Inscription b.d. illegible.
Uncompleted work.
(L'Atelier de Renoir, foreword by A. André and
M. Elder, 2 vol., Paris 1931, No. 429, pl. 138,
as uncompleted, painted ap. 1911-1915).
Attributed to the Louvre Museum by the Private
Properties Office, 1950.

F.R. 1943-63
READER IN WHITE
T. H. 0.257; W. 0.205.
S.h.g.: Renoir.
Painted in 1915 or 1916.
Berthellemy donation, with reservation of usufruct,
1930; entered the Louvre Museum 1943.
Cat. impr. 379 — S.A.I. 1616 — C.P.t.l. p. 321.

F.R. 1951-15
ODALISQUE SLEEPING, also known as ODALISQUE
WITH BABOUCHES

T. H. 0.50; W. 0.53.
S.b.g.: Renoir.
Painted ap. 1915-1917.
Presented by Dr and Mme Albert Charpentier, 1951.
Cat. impr. 378 — S.A.I. 1615 — C.P.t.l. p. 321.

F.R. 2795
WOMEN BATHING
T. H. 1.10; W. 1.60.
Painted in 1918 or 1919.
Presented by the artist's sons, 1923.
Cat. impr. 380 — S.A.I. 1617 — C.P.t.l. p. 319.

F.R. 1945-5
LANDSCAPE. Design for a tapestry.
T. H. 0.385; W. 0.460.
S.b.g. Renoir.
Acquired in 1945.
Cat. impr. 367 — S.A.I. 1612 — C.P.t.l. p. 321.

F.R. 2745
THE GREAT JUDGEMENT OF PARIS
Original plaster: H. 0.76; W. 0.94.
1914, with the collaboration of R. Guino.
Acquired in 1954, on deposit from the department
of sculptures.
Cat. impr. 453.

ROUART Henri
Paris, 1833-1912

F.R. 3832
THE TERRACE BY THE SEINE AT MELUN
T. H. 0.465; W. 0.655.
S.b.g.: H. Rouart.
Painted ap. 1880.
Acquired 1934.
Cat. impr. 381 — S.A.I. 1658 — C.P.t.l. p. 336.

INV. 3617
THE CHURCH OF SAN MICHAEL, NEAR VENICE
T. H. 0.61; W. 0.50.
S.d. on the boat: H. Rouart.
Painted ap. 1883.
Presented by Ernest Rouart, the artist's son, 1932.
Cat. impr. 382 — S.A.I. 1659 — C.P.t.l. p. 336.

ROUSSEAU Henri, also known as Le Douanier
Laval, 1844 - Paris, 1910.

WAR, also known as THE RIDE OF DISCORD
T. H. 1.14; W. 1.95.
S.b.d.: Henri Rousseau.
Painted in 1894.
(Bouret 7, Vallier 69).
Acquired 1946.
Cat. impr. 383 — S.A.I. 1663 — C.P.t.l. p. 336.

F.R. 1965-15
PORTRAIT OF A WOMAN, Clémence Boitard,
the artist's first wife.
T. H. 1.98; W. 1.15.
S.b.g.: Henri Rousseau.
Ap. 1897.
(Bouret 66; Vallier 101).
Presented by Baroness Eva Gebhard-Gourgaud,
1965.
C.P.t.l. p. 337.

F.R. 1937-7
THE SNAKE-CHARMER
T. H. 1.690; W. 1.895.
S.D.b.d.: Henri-Julien Rousseau, 1907.
(Bouret 34; Vallier 200).
Jacques Doucet bequest, 1936.
Cat. impr. 384 — S.A.I. 1664 — C.P.t.l. p. 336.

ROUSSEAU Théodore
Paris, 1812 - Barbizon (Seine-et-Marne), 1867.

F.R. 1961-24
MORNING
B. H. 0.418; W. 0.643.
S.b.g.: Th. Rousseau.
Eduardo Mollard donation, 1961.
C.P.t.l. p. 340.

SEURAT Georges-Pierre
Paris, 1859-1891

F.R. 1973-23
OUTSKIRTS OF A FOREST IN SPRING
B. H. 0.165; W. 0.26.
Painted ap. 1882-83.
(Dorra et Rewald 54; De Hauke 51).
M. and R. Kaganovitch donation, 1973.

F.R. 1965-13
STUDY FOR "BATHING AT ASNIÈRES"
B. H. 0.155; W. 0.250.
Painted 1883.
Study for the painting in the National Gallery
in London.
(Dorra et Rewald 91; De Hauke 84).
Presented by Baroness Eva Gebhard-Gourgaud,
1965.
C.P.t.l. p. 345.

F.R. 1948-1
STUDY FOR "SUNDAY AFTERNOON AT THE ILE
DE LA GRANDE JATTE"
B. H. 0.155; W. 0.250.
Painted 1884.
Study for the painting in the Art Institute of Chicago.
(Dorra et Rewald 126; De Hauke 109).
Presented by T. and G.-H. Rivière in memory
of their parents, 1948.
S.A.I. 1716 — C.P.t.l. p. 345.

F.R. 2828
STUDY FOR "SUNDAY AFTERNOON
AT THE ILE DE LA GRANDE JATTE"
B. H. 0.16; W. 0.25.
Study for a detail of the painting executed between
1884 and 1886 (Art Institute, Chicago).
(Dorra et Rewald 129; De Hauke 129).
Anonymous gift, 1930.
Cat. impr. 386 — S.A.I. 1717 — C.P.t.l. p. 344.

F.R. 1947-13
MODEL, FULL-FACE
B. H. 0.25; W. 0.16.
S.b.d.: Seurat.
Painted 1886-87.
Study for "Models" (Barnes Foundation, Merion,
Penn.).
Dorra et Rewald 174; De Hauke 183).
Acquired 1947.
Cat. impr. 387 — S.A.I. 1718 — C.P.t.l. p. 345.

F.R. 1947-14
MODEL, PROFILE
B. H. 0.25; W. 0.16.
Painted 1886-87.
Study for "Models" (Barnes Foundation, Nerion,
Penn).
(Dorra et Rewald 175; De Hauke 182).
Acquired in 1047.
Cat. impr. 389 — S.A.I. 1719 — C.P.t.l. p. 345.

F.R. 1947-15
MODEL, BACK-VIEW
B. H. 0.245; W. 0.155.
Painted 1886-87.
Study for "Models" (Barnes Foundation, Merion,
Penn').
(Dorra et Rewald 176; De Hauke 181).
Acquired 1947.
Cat. impr. 388 — S.A.I. 1720 — C.P.t.l. p. 345.

F.R. 1952-1
PORT-EN-BESSIN. OUTER HARBOUR. HIGH
TIDE (Calvados).
T. H. 0.67; W. 0.82.
Painted 1888.
(De Hauke 193).
Acquired with deferred payments from an
anonymous gift from Canada, 1952.
Cat. impr. 390 — S.A.I. 1721 — C.P.t.l. p. 345.

F.R. 1937-123
SKETCH FOR "THE CIRCUS"
T. H. 0.55; W. 0.46.
Painted 1891.
(Dorra et Rewald 210; De Hauke 212).
Presented by Mme J. Doucet according to the wish
expressed by her husband, 1937.
Cat. impr. 391 — S.A.I. 1722.

F.R. 2511
THE CIRCUS
T. H. 1.855; W. 1.525.
Painted 1891.
(Dorra et Rewald 211; De Hauke 213).
Bequeathed by John Quinn, 1924; entered 1927.
Cat. impr. 392 — S.A.I. 1723 — C.P.t.l. p. 344.

SIGNAC Paul
Paris 1863-1935

F.R. 1968-3
A PARIS SUBURB
T. H. 0.729; W. 0.916.
Inscr. S.D.b.d.: ... A ... chy, P. Signac 83 (partially
effaced).
Acquired 1968.
C.P.t.l. p. 347.

F.R. 1958-1
RIVER-BANKS. THE SEINE AT HERBLAY
(Val-d'Oise).
S.D.b.g.: P. Signac, 89. Inscr. b.d.: Op. 208.
Acquired with the participation of Mme Cachin-
Signac, the artist's daughter, and an anonymous
art-collector, 1958.
Cat. impr. 393 — S.A.I. 1728 — C.P.t.l. p. 347.

F.R. 1976-78
WOMAN READING BY LAMP-LIGHT
B. H. 0.245; W. 0.152.
Painted 1890.

(An urban landscape sketched on the back).
Presented by Mme Ginette Signac, with
reservation of usufruct, 1976.

F.R. 1957-12
THE RED BUOY
T. H. 0.81; W. 0.65.
S.D.b.d.: 95 P. Signac.
Presented by Dr. P. Hébert, with reservation
of usufruct, 1957; entered 1973.

F.R. 1976-77
THE GREEN SAIL, VENICE
T. H. 0.65; W. 0.81.
S.D.b.g.: P. Signac/1904.
Presented by Mme Ginette Signac, with reservation
of usufruct, 1976.

*Other works by Signac, on exhibition in the Palais
de Tokyo and not listed here, have been trans-
mitted by the National Museum of Modern Art.*

SISLEY Alfred
Paris, 1839 - Moret-sur-Loing (Seine-et-Marne),
1899.

F.R. 1971-15
HERON WITH SPREAD WINGS
T. H. 0.80; W. 1.00.
S.b.d.: Sisley.
Painted ap. 1865-67.
(Daulte 5).
Presented by Mme P. Goujon, with reservation
of usufruct; entered 1972.

F.R. 1951-40
VIEW OF THE SAINT-MARTIN CANAL, Paris.
T. H. 0.50; W. 0.65.
S.D.b.d.: Sisley, 1870.
1870 *Salon.*
(Daulte 16).
Presented by Paul Gachet, 1951.
Cat. impr. 394 — S.A.I. 1729 — C.P.t.l. p. 351.

F.R. 1701
THE SAINT-MARTIN CANAL, Paris.
T. H. 0.380; W. 0.465.
S.D.b.d.: Sisley, 72.
(Daulte 35).
Etienne Moreau-Nélaton donation, 1907.
Brière M. 94 — Cat. impr. 395 — S.A.I. 1731.
C.P.t.l. p. 348.

F.R. 1692
RUE DE LA CHAUSSÉE AT ARGENTEUIL,
also known as SQUARE AT ARGENTEUIL
T. H. 0.465; W. 0.660.
S.D.b.d.: Sisley, 1872.
(Daulte 31).
Etienne Moreau-Nélaton donation, 1906.
Brière M. 92 — Cat. impr. 398 — S.A.I. 1732.
C.P.t.l. p. 348.

F.R. 1688
THE FOOTBRIDGE AT ARGENTEUIL
T. H. 0.39; W. 0.60.
S.D.b.d.: A. Sisley, 1872.
(Daulte 32).
Etienne Moreau-Nélaton donation, 1906.
Brière M. 91 — Cat. impr. 397 — S.A.I. 1730.
C.P.t.l. p. 348.

F.R. 2435
ILE SAINT-DENIS
T. H. 0.505; W. 0.650.
S.b. towards the l.: Sisley.
Painted 1872.
(Daulte 47).
Presented by Ernest May, with reservation of usu-
fruct, 1923; entered the Louvre Museum, 1926.
Cat. impr. 405 — S.A.I. 1733 — C.P.t.l. p. 350.

FR 1937-63
THE ILE DE LA GRANDE-JATTE (Neuilly-sur-Seine)
T. H. 0.505; W. 0.650.
S.D.b.g.: Sisley 73.
(Daulte 66).
Antonin Personnaz bequest, 1937.
Cat. impr. 402 — S.A.I. 1726 — C.P.t.l. p. 350.

M.N.R. 208
THE SEINE AT BOUGIVAL
T. H. 0.460; W. 0.653.
S.b.g.: Sisley.
Painted 1873.
(Daulte 87).
Attributed to the Louvre Museum by the Private
Properties Office, 1951.
S.A.I. 1738 — C.P.t.l. p. 351.

F.R. 1690
BOATS AT THE BOUGIVAL LOCK
T. H. 0.460; W. 0.65.
S.D.b.d.: Sisley, 73.
(Daulte 90).
Etienne Moreau-Nélaton donation, 1906.
Brière M. 95 — Cat. impr. 399 — S.A.I. 1734.
C.P.t.l. p. 348.

F.R. 2079
THE ROAD. VIEW OF THE SÈVRES ROAD,
Louveciennes.
T. H. 0.547; W. 0.730.
S.D.b.g.: Sisley, 73.
(Daulte 102).
Presented by Joanny Paytel, with reservation
of usufruct, 1914; usufruct abandoned, 1918.
Cat. impr. 401 — S.A.I. 1737 — C.P.t.l. p. 349.

F.R. 1937-65
LOUVECIENNES. HILL-TOPS AT MARLY
T. H. 0.380; W. 0.465.
S.b.d.: Sisley.
Doubtless painted in 1873.
(Daulte 83).
Antonin Personnaz bequest, 1937.
Cat. impr. 400 — S.A.I. 1735 — C.P.t.l. p. 351.

F.R. 2787
REGATTA AT MOSELY (near Hampton Court,
England)
T. H. 0.660; W. 0.915.
Painted 1874.
(Daulte 126).
Gustave Caillebotte bequest, 1894; entered 1896.
Cat. impr. 406 — S.A.I. 1741 — C.P.t.l. p. 350.

F.R. 1937-64
FOG AT VOISINS
T. H. 0.505; W. 0.650.
S.D.b.d.: Sisley, 74.
(Daulte 137).
Antonin Personnaz bequest, 1937.
Cat. impr. 412 — S.A.I. 1740 — C.P.t.l. p. 351.

F.R. 2019
THE VILLAGE OF VOISINS
T. H. 0.380; W. 0.465.
S.D.b.g.: Sisley, 74.
(Daulte 142).
Camondo bequest, 1911.
Brière CA. 199 — Cat. impr. 404 — S.A.I. 1739.
C.P.t.l. p. 349.

F.R. 1691
SNOW AT MARLY-LE-ROI
T. H. 0.465; W. 0.560.
S.D.b.d.: Sisley, 75.
(Daulte 193).
Etienne Moreau-Nélaton donation, 1906.
Brière M. 97 — Cat. impr. 408 — S.A.I. 1743.
C.P.t.l. p. 348.

F.R. 1689
THE FORGE AT MARLY-LE-ROI
T. H. 0.550; W. 0.735.
S.D.b.d.: Sisley, 75.
(Daulte 183).
Etienne Moreau-Nélaton donation, 1906.
Brière M. 96 — Cat. impr. 407 — S.A.I. 1742.
C.P.t.l. p. 348.

F.R. 1973-24
THE VERSAILLES ROAD
T. H. 0.47; W. 0.38.
S.D.b.d.: Sisley, 75.
(Daulte 162).
M. and R. Kaganovitch donation, 1973.

F.R. 2021
BOAT IN THE FLOOD (Port-Marly)
T. H. 0.505; W. 0.610.
S.D.b.d.: Sisley 76.
(Daulte 239).
Camondo bequest, 1911.
Brière CA. 201 — Cat. impr. 409 — S.A.I. 1744.
C.P.t.l. p. 349.

F.R. 2020
FLOOD AT PORT-MARLY
T. H. 0.60; W. 0.81.
S.D.b.g.: Sisley, 76.
(Daulte 240).
Camondo bequest, 1911.
Brière CA. 200 — Cat. impr. 411 — S.A.I. 1745.
C.P.t.l. p. 349.

F.R. 1972-34
IN THE SNOW. A FARM-YARD
AT MARLY-LE-ROI
T. H. 0.385; W. 0.555.
S.D.b.d.: Sisley, 76.
(Daulte 197).
Eduardo Mollard bequest, 1972.

F.R. 2786
THE SEINE AT SURESNES
T. H. 0.607; W. 0.737.
S.D.b.g.: Sisley, 77.
(Daulte 267).
Gustave Caillebotte bequest, 1894; entered 1896.
Cat. impr. 413 — S.A.I. 1746 — C.P.t.l. p. 350.

F.R. 1951-12
THE ROAD TO LOUVECIENNES UNDER SNOW
T. H. 0.460; W. 0.555.
S.b.d.: Sisley.

Painted ap. 1877-78.
(Daulte 281).
Presented by Dr. and Mme Albert Charpentier,
1951.
Cat. impr. 403 — S.A.I. 1749 — C.P.t.l. p. 351.

F.R. 2022
SNOW AT LOUVECIENNES
T. H. 0.610; W. 0.505.
S.D.b.d.: Sisley, 78.
(Daulte 282).
Camondo bequest, 1911.
Brière CA. 203 — Cat. impr. 414 — S.A.I. 1748.
C.P.t.l. p. 349.

F.R. 1693
RESTING BY THE BROOK. AT THE EDGE
OF THE WOOD
T. H. 0.735; W. 0.805.
S.D.b.d.: Sisley, 78 (not 72).
(Daulte 42).
Etienne Moreau-Nélaton donation, 1906.
Brière M. 93 — Cat. impr. 396 — S.A.I. 1747.
C.P.t.l. p. 348.

M.N.R. 193
A RAINY SPRING IN THE OUTSKIRTS OF PARIS
H. 0.46; W. 0.55.
S.D.b.g.: Sisley 79.
(Daulte 306).
Attributed to the Louvre Museum by the Private
Properties Office, 1950.

F.R. 2025
SNOW AT VENEUX-NADON
T. H. 0.55; W. 0.74.
S.b.d.: Sisley.
Painted 1880.
(Daulte 401).
Camondo bequest, 1911.
Brière CA. 204 — Cat. impr. 416 — S.A.I. 1751,
C.P.t.l. p. 349.

F.R. 2784
SKIRT OF A FOREST IN SPRING
T. H. 0.605; W. 0.735.
S.D.b.d.: Sisley, 80.
(Daulte 350).
Gustave Caillebotte bequest, 1894; entered 1896.
Cat. impr. 415 — S.A.I. 1750 — C.P.t.l. p. 350.

M.N.R. 210 bis
THE SEINE FROM THE HILLSIDE AT BY
T. H. 0.37; W. 0.55.
S.b.g. and b.d. (twice): Sisley.
Painted 1881.
(Daulte 443).
Attributed to the Louvre Museum by the Private
Properties Office, 1950.
Cat. impr. 419 — S.A.I. 1752 — C.P.t.l. p. 351.

F.R. 2026
EDGE OF A WOOD AT SABLONS, also known as
AT THE EDGE OF THE WOOD (edge of the Forest
of Fontainebleau, near Moret-sur-Loing).
T. H. 0.605; W. 0.735.
S.b.d.: Sisley.
Painted 1883.
(Daulte 502).
Camondo bequest, 1911.
Brière CA. 202 — Cat. impr. 410 — S.A.I. 1753.
C.P.t.l. p. 349.

F.R. 2700
FARM-YARD AT SAINT-MAMMÈS
T. H. 0.735; W. 0.930.
S.D.b.d.: Sisley, 84.
(Daulte 544).
Gustave Caillebotte bequest, 1894; entered 1896.
Cat. impr. 418 — S.A.I. 1754 — C.P.t.l. p. 350.

F.R. 1972-33
THE LOING CANAL
T. H. 0.385; W. 0.55.
S.D.b.d.: Sisley 84.
(Daulte 522).
Edouardo Mollard bequest, 1972.

F.R. 2785
SAINT-MAMMÈS
T. H. 0.545; W. 0.735.
S.D.b.g.: Sisley, 85.
(Daulte 629).
Gustave Caillebotte bequest, 1894; entered 1896.
Cat. impr. 417 — S.A.I. 1755 — C.P.t.l. p. 350.

F.R. 2023
ASPENS AND ACACIAS
T. H. 0.60; W. 0.73.
S.D.b.d.: Sisley, 89.
(Daulte 712).
Camondo bequest, 1911.
Brière CA. 205 — Cat. impr. 420 — S.A.I. 1756.
C.P.t.l. p. 349.

F.R. 2024
MORET, BY THE LOING RIVER
T. H. 0.605; W. 0.730.
S.D.b.d.: Sisley, 92.
(Daulte 815).
Camondo bequest, 1911.
Brière CA. 206 — Cat. impr. 421 — S.A.I. 1757.
C.P.t.l. p. 349.

INV. 20723
THE LOING CANAL
T. H. 0.73; W. 0.93.
S.D.b.d.: Sisley, 92.
(Daulte 816).
Presented by some of the artist's friends, 1899.
(Painting formerly inventoried by error F.R. 2699).
Cat. impr. 422 — S.A.I. 1758 — C.P.t.l. p. 350.

F.R. 1972-35
THE BRIDGE AT MORET
T. H. 0.735; W. 0.923.
S.D.b.g.: Sisley, 93.
(Daulte 817).
Eduardo Mollard bequest, 1972.

STEVENS Alfred
Brussels, 1823 - Paris, 1906

F.R. 1972-36
A FAMILY SCENE
T. H. 0.515; W. 0.653.
S.b.d.: A. Stevens.
Eduardo Mollard bequest, 1972.

TOULOUSE-LAUTREC Henri de
Albi, 1864 - Château de Malromé (Gironde), 1901.

F.R. 1947-32
HENRY SAMARY (1865-1902), of the Comédie-

Française.
C. H. 0.749; W. 0.519.
S.D.b.d.: H. T. Lautrec/89
(the initials H.T.L.
intertwined to form a monogram).
(Dortu P. 330).
Presented by M. Jacques Laroche with
reservation of usufruct, 1947; entered 1976.

F.R. 1937-36
WOMAN COMBING HER HAIR
Carton. H. 0.44; W. 0.30.
S.h.g.: H.T. Lautrec (H.T.L. intertwined).
Painted 1891.
(Dortu P. 390).
Antonin Personnaz bequest, 1937.
Cat. impr. 434 — S.A.I. 1789 — C.P.t.l. p. 362.

F.R. 1959-3
JUSTINE DIEUHL
WOMAN SEATED IN A GARDEN
Carton. H. 0.74; W. 0.58.
S.B. towards the r.: H.T. Lautrec (H.T.L.
intertwined).
Painted ap. 1891.
(Dortu P. 394).
Ex-collection Masukata. Entered the Louvre
Museum 1959, in accordance with the Peace
Treaty with Japan.
Cat. impr. 423 — S.A.I. 1777 — C.P.t.l. p. 362.

F.R. 1953-29
WOMAN WITH GLOVES (Honorine Platzer).
Carton. H. 0.54; W. 0.40.
S.h.d.: H.T. (H.T.L. intertwined).
Painted 1891.
(Dortu P. 396).
Presented by the Society of Friends of the Louvre
Museum, 1953.
Cat. impr. 424 — S.A.I. 1778 — C.P.t.l. p. 362.

INV. 20140
WOMAN WITH A BLACK FEATHER BOA
Carton. H. 0.53; W. 0.41.
S.b.d.: H.T. Lautrec (H.T.L. interwined).
Painted 1892.
(Dortu P. 435).
Presented by Comtesse Alphonse
de Toulouse Lautrec, the artist's mother, 1902.
Cat. impr. 425 — S.A.I. 1779 — C.P.t.l. p. 361.

F.R. 1937-37
JANE AVRIL DANCING (1868-1923).
Carton. H. 855; W. 0.450.
S.h towards the r.: H.T. Lautrec (H.T.L.
intertwined).
Painted ap. 1892.
(Dortu P. 416).
Antonin Personnaz bequest, 1937.
Cat. impr. 426 — S.A.I. 1780 — C.P.t.l. p. 362.

F.R. 1937-38
IN BED
Carton on a cradled panel. H. 0.540; W. 0.705.
S.h. towards the r.: H.T. Lautrec (H.T.L.
intertwined).
Painted ap. 1892.
(Dortu P. 439).
Antonin Personnaz bequest, 1937.
Cat. impr. 427 — S.A.I. 1781 — C.P.t.l. p. 362.

F.R. 1943-66

WOMAN PULLING ON HER STOCKING,
also known as WOMAN IN A BROTHEL
Carton. H. 0.58; W. 0.46.
S.b.d.: H.T. Lautrec (intertwined monogram.
Doubtful).
Painted ap. 1894.
(Dortu P. 552).
Presented by A. Berthellemy with reservation
of usufruct, 1930; entered 1943.
Cat. impr. 428 — S.A.I. 1782 — C.P.t.l. p. 362.

F.R. 1943-65
BLONDE WOMAN IN A BROTHEL
Carton. H. 0.69; W. 0.485.
S.B. towards the l.: H.T. (H.T.L. intertwined).
Study for "In the salon of the rue des Moulins"
(Albi Museum).
Painted in 1894.
(Dortu P. 555).
Presented by A. Berthellemy, with reservation of
usufruct, 1930; entered the Louvre Museum 1943.
Cat. impr. 429 — S.A.I. 1783 — C.P.t.l. p. 362.

F.R. 2027
THE CLOWNESS CHA-U-KO, performer at
the Moulin-Rouge.
Carton. H. 0.64; W. 0.49.
S.D.b.d.: H.T. Lautrec, 95 (H.T.L. intertwined).
(Dortu P. 581).
Camondo bequest, 1911.
Brière CA. 207 — Cat. impr. 430 — S.A.I. 1784.
C.P.t.l. p. 361.

F.R. 2826
PANELS FOR LA GOULUE'S STAND AT THE
FOIRE DU TRONE IN PARIS

MOORISH WOMEN DANCING, also known as
LES ALMÉES DANCE
T. H. 2.850; W. 3.075.
D.b. towards the r.: 1895.
(Dortu P. 591).

DANCE AT THE MOULIN-ROUGE
(LA GOULUE AND BONELESS VALENTIN)
T. H. 2.98; W. 3.16.
S.b.d.: H.T.L. (intertwined monogram).
Painted 1895.
(Dortu P. 592).
Acquired, cut up into eight panels, with several
falls of canvas in 1929; except for the fragment of
"Valentin le Désossé", presented by M. Auffray,
1929. Reco Cat. impr. 431 — S.A.I. 1785 and 1786.
C.P.t.l. p. 361.

F.R. 1937-39
WOMAN IN PROFILE (MADAME LUCY)
Carton. H. 0.56; W. 0.48.
S. towards b.l.: H.T. Lautrec (H.T.L. intertwined).
Painted 1896.
(Dortu P. 608).
Antonin Personnaz bequest, 1937.
Cat. impr. 432 — S.A.I. 1787 — C.P.t.l. p. 362

F.R. 2242
WOMAN AT HER TOILET
Carton. H. 0.67; W. 0.54.
S.b.d.: Lautrec (beginning illegible)
Painted 1896.
(Dortu P. 610).
Bequeathed by Pierre Goujon, 1914.
Cat. impr. 433 — S.A.I. 1788 — C.P.t.l. p. 361.

F.R. 2281
PAUL LECLERQ (1872-1956), a friend of the artist,
founder of "La Revue Blanche"
Carton. H. 0.54; W. 0.67.
Painted 1897.
(Dortu P. 645).
Presented by Paul Leclerq, 1920.
Brière 3148 — Cat. impr. 435 — S.A.I. 1790.
C.P.t.l. p. 361.

F.R. 1943-64
LOUIS BOUGLÉ, a friend of the artist.
B. H. 0.63; W. 0.51.
S.b.g.: HT (intertwined monogram).
Painted 1898.
(Dortu P. 660).
Presented by A. Berthellemy, with reservation of
usufruct, 1930; entered the Louvre Museum 1943.
Cat. impr. 436 — S.A.I. 1791 — C.P.t.l. p. 362.

VAN GOGH Vincent

Groot-Zundert (Brabant), 1853 - Auvers-sur-Oise,
1890.

F.R. 1954-20
HEAD OF A PEASANT-WOMAN FROM HOLLAND
T. H. 0.385; W. 0.265.
Painted in in 1884.
Study for "The potatoe-eaters".
(La Faille 134; La Faille Hypérion 143).
Acquired 1954.
Cat. impr. 142 — S.A.I. 1948 — C.P.t.l. p. 383.

F.R. 1989
FRITILLARIES IN A COPPER VASE
T. H. 0.730; W. 0.605.
S.h.g.: Vincent.
Painted in 1886.
(La Faille 213. La Faille Hypérion 298).
Camondo bequest, 1911.
Brière CA. 208 — Cat. impr. 143 — S.A.I. 1949 —
C.P.t.l. p. 381.

F.R. 2243
LA GUINGUETTE ("Le Billard en bois", later named
"A la bonne franquette", in Montmartre).
T. H. 0.495; W. 0.645.
S.b.g.: Vincent.
Painted in 1886.
(La Faille 238; La Faille Hypérion 393).
Bequeathed by Pierre Goujon, 1914.
Cat. impr. 144 — S.A.I. 1950 — C.P.t.l. p. 381.

F.R. 2325
RESTAURANT DE LA SIRÈNE, at Asnières.
T. H. 0.545; W. 0.655.
Painted in 1887.
(La Faille 313; La Faille Hypérion 375).
Bequeathed by Joseph Reinach, 1921.
Cat. impr. 145 — S.A.I. 1951 — C.P.t.l. p. 381.

F.R. 1965-14
ITALIAN WOMAN (Agostina Segatori, owner
of the Paris cabaret "Le Tambourin".
T. H. 0.81; W. 0.60.
Painted in 1887.
(La Faille 381; La Faille Hypérion 285).
Presented by Baroness Eva Gebhard-Gourgaud,
1965.
C.P.t.l. p. 383.

F.R. 1947-28
SELF-PORTRAIT
T. H. 0.44; W. 0.351.
Painted in Paris, autumn 1887.
(La Faille 320; La Faille Hypérion 400).
Presented by M. Jacques Laroche with reservation
of usufruct, 1947; entered 1976.

F.R. 3670
A GYPSY ENCAMPMENT, near Arles.
T. H. 0.45; W. 0.51.
Painted August 1888.
(La Faille 445; La Faille Hypérion 487).
Bequeathed by M. and Mme Raymond Koechlin,
1931.
Cat. impr. 146 — S.A.I. 1952 — C.P.t.l. p. 381.

F.R. 1944-9
EUGÈNE BOCH (1855-1941), Belgian painter
T. H. 0.60; W. 0.45.
Painted September 1888.
(La Faille 462; La Faille Hypérion 490).
Bequeathed by Eugène Bosch through the
intermediary of the Society of Friends of the Louvre
Museum, 1941; entered 1944.
Cat. impr. 147 — S.A.I. 1953 — C.P.t.l. p. 382.

F.R. 1952-6
L'ARLÉSIENNE
T. H. 0.923; W. 0.735.
Painted in 1888.
(La Faille 489; La Faille Hypérion XI).
Presented by Mme Goldschmidt-Rothschild,
born Marianne de Friedlander-Fuld, August 1944,
with reservation of usufruct; entered 1974.

F.R. 1950-9
THE DANCE-HALL AT ARLES
T. H. 0.65; W. 0.81.
Painted in 1888.
(La Faille 547; La Faille Hypérion 555).
Presented by M. and Mme André Meyer with
reservation of usufruct, 1950; entered 1975.

F.R. 1949-17
SELF-PORTRAIT
T. H. 0.650; W. 0.545.
Painted in 1889.
(La Faille 627; La Faille Hypérion 748).
Presented by Paul and Marguerite Gachet, 1949.
Cat. impr. 156 — S.A.I. 1962 — C.P.t.l. p. 382.

F.R. 1959-2
VAN GOGH'S BEDROOM AT ARLES
T. H. 0.575; W. 0.740.
Painted September 1889.
A replica of the picture painted in Arles in October
1888 (Chicago Arts Institute).
(La Faille 483; La Faille Hypérion 628).
Ex-collection Matsukata. Entered the Louvre Museum
in 1959, in accordance with the Peace Treaty with
Japan.
Cat. impr. 153 — S.A.I. 1954 — C.P.t.l. p. 383.

F.R. 1973-25
SAINT-PAUL'S HOSPITAL AT SAINT-RÉMY
T. H. 0.63; W. 0.48.
Painted October 1889.
(La Faille 653; La Faille Hypérion 666).
M. and R. Kaganovitch donation, 1973.

F.R. 1952-17
NOON, also known as THE SIESTA (after Millet).
T. H. 0.73; W. 0.91.
Painted December 1889-January 1890, after a wood
engraving by Jacques-Adrien Lavieille reproducing
one of J.-F. Millet's drawings of "Four hours of the
day".
(La Faille 686; La Faille Hypérion p. 677).
Presented by Mme Fernand Halpen with reservation
of usufruct, 1952; entered 1963.
C.P.t.l. p. 382.

F.R. 1954-15
DR. GACHET'S GARDEN AT AUVERS-SUR-OISE
T. H. 0.73; W. 0.52.
Painted May 27, 1890.
(La Faille 755; La Faille Hypérion p. 557).
Presented by Paul Gachet, 1954.
Cat. impr. 148 — S.A.I. 1955 — C.P.t.l. p. 382.

F.R. 1949-16
DR. PAUL GACHET (1828-1909).
T. H. 0.68; W. 0.57.
Painted June 1890.
(La Faille 754; La Faille Hypérion 753).
Presented by Paul and Marguerite Gachet,
the subject's children, 1949.
Cat. impr. 155 — S.A.I. 1961 — C.P.t.l. p. 382.

F.R. 1954-13
MADEMOISELLE GACHET IN HER GARDEN,
Marguerite Gachet (1871-1949).
Dr. Gachet's daughter.
T. H. 0.460; W. 0.555.
Painted June 1st 1890.
(La Faille 756; La Faille Hypérion p. 557).
Presented by Paul Gachet, the model's brother.
1954.
Cat. impr. 149 — S.A.I. 1956 — C.P.t.l. p. 382.

F.R. 1951-42.
THE CHURCH AT AUVERS-SUR-OISE
T. H. 0.940; W. 0.745.
Painted June 1890.
(La Faille 789; La Faille Hypérion 557).
Acquired with the help of Paul Gachet and
an anonymous donation from Canada, 1951.
Cat. impr. 150 — S.A.I. 1957 — C.P.t.l. p. 382.

F.R. 1954-12
ROSES AND ANEMONES
T. H. 0.517; W. 0.520.
Painted June 1890.
(La Faille 764; La Faille Hypérion 557).
Presented by Paul Gachet, 1954.
Cat. impr. 151 — S.A.I. 1958 — C.P.t.l. p. 382.

F.R. 1954-16
TWO LITTLE GIRLS
T. H. 0.512; W. 0.510.
Painted June 1890.
(La Faille 783; La Faille Hypérion 773).
Presented by Paul Gachet, 1954.
Cat. impr. 152 — S.A.I. 1959 — C.P.t.l. p. 383.

F.R. 1954-14
THATCHED COTTAGES AT CORDEVILLE,
AUVERS-SUR-OISE, formerly known as
THATCHED COTTAGES AT MONTCEL
T. H. 0.73; W. 0.92.
Painted June 1890.
(La Faille 792; La Faille Hypérion 779).

Presented by Paul Gachet, 1954.
Cat. impr. 154 — S.A.I. 1960 — C.P.t.l. p. 382.

VAN RYSSEL Paul,
pseudonym of Dr. Paul Gachet
Lille, 1828 - Auvers-sur-Oise, 1909.

F.R. 1954-28
THE OLD ROAD AT AUVERS-SUR-OISE
T. H. 0.405; W. 0.545.
S.D.b.d.: P. Gachet, 81.
Presented by Paul Gachet, the artist's son, 1954.
Cat. impr. 385 — S.A.I. 1963 — C.P.t.l. p. 386.

F.R. 1958-16
APPLES
Carton. H. 0.27; W. 0.35.
S. towards b.d.: V.R.
Acquired in 1958.
Cat. impr. 385a — S.A.I. 1964 — C.P.t.l. p. 386.

VIGNON Victor
Villers-Cotterêts (Aisne), 1847 - Meulan (Yvelines), 1909.

F.R. 2794
LANDSCAPE AT AUVERS-SUR-OISE.
HOUSES IN THE VALLEY
T. H. 0.335; W. 0.415.
S.b. towards the left: V. Vignon.
Painted ap. 1880-85.
Presented by MM. Bernheim-Jeune, 1911.
(reinventoried by error F.R. 3930).
Cat. impr. 438 — S.A.I. 1983 — C.P.t.l. p. 394.

F.R. 1953-36
THE CHEMIN DES FRILEUSES AT EVECQUEMONT
(Yvelines)
T. H. 0.46; W. 0.65.
S.b.d.: V. Vignon.
Painted ap. 1880-85.
Presented by André Kahn, 1953.
Cat. impr. 437 — S.A.I. 1982 — C.P.t.l. p. 394.

VLAMINCK Maurice de
Paris, 1876 - Rueil, 1958.

F.R. 1973-26
RESTAURANT AT MARLY-LE-ROI
T. H. 0.60; W. 0.815.
S.b.d.: Vlaminck.
Painted ap. 1905.
M. and R. Kaganovitch donation, 1973.

F.R. 1973-27
STILL-LIFE
T. H. 0.54; W. 0.645.
S.b.d.: Vlaminck.
Painted ap. 1910.
M. and R. Kaganovitch donation, 1973.

Hélène and Victor Lyon Donation

On exhibition at the Louvre Museum.

BOUDIN. Sailing-boats. Camaret. 1872.

CÉZANNE, L'Estaque. ap. 1871.

FANTIN-LATOUR. Flowers 1872.

BOUDIN. The harbour at Trouville. 1891.

JONGKIND. Notre-Dame de Paris. 1854.

JONGKIND. Landscape. 1857.

JONGKIND. Skaters. 1864.

JONGKIND. Entry to the harbour at Honfleur. 1866.

JONGKIND. The Canal. 1877.

LINDON. Still-life.

MONET. In the region of Honfleur. Snow.
1867.

PISSARRO. View of Pontoise. 1877.

MONET. Drift-ice on the Seine at Bougival.
ap. 1867?

MONET. The break-up near Vétheuil. 1880.

PISSARRO. The watering-place.
Eragny. 1895.

RENOIR. Girls reading. ap. 1890-95.

RENOIR. Portrait of a woman.

RENOIR. Portrait of a woman
seated. ap. 1916-18.

SISLEY. La route de Mantes. 1874.

SISLEY. Saint-Cloud. 1877.

SISLEY. The wood
at Les Roches. 1880.

TOULOUSE-LAUTREC.
G.-L. Dennery. ap. 1883.

Hélène and Victor Lyon Donation

with reservation of usufruct, 1961; entered in 1977
*(in accordance with the wishes of the donators these works are exhibited
in the Louvre Museum together with the old paintings that constitute the collection).*

BOUDIN Eugène

F.R. 1961-31
SAILING-BOATS, CAMARET
T. H. 0.50; W. 0.76.
S.D.b.d.: Boudin 72?
(Schmit 796).

R.F. 1961-30
THE HARBOUR AT TROUVILLE
T. H. 0.41; W. 0.555.
S.D.b.g.: E. Boudin/Trouville 91.
(Schmit 2849).

CÉZANNE Paul

F.R. 1961-34
L'ESTAQUE. STUDY IN EVENING
T. H. 0.435; W. 0.595.
Painted ap. 1871?
(Venturi 57).

FANTIN-LATOUR Henri

F.R. 1961-39
FLOWERS
T. H. 0.315; W. 0.24.
S.D.h.g.: Fantin 72.
(Fantin-Latour 632?).

JONGKIND Johan-Barthold

F.R. 1961-52
NOTRE-DAME DE PARIS
T. H. 0.27; W. 0.405.
S.D.b.d.: Jongkind 54.

F.R. 1961-51
LANDSCAPE
T. H. 0.42; W. 0.56.
S.D.b.d.: Jongkind, 57.
(Hefting 167).

F.R. 1961-54
SKATERS
T. H. 0.425; W. 0.56.
S.D.b.d.: Jongkind, 1864.

F.R. 1961-51
ENTRY OF THE HARBOUR AT HONFLEUR
T. H. 0.425; W. 0.565.
S.D.b.g.: Jongkind, 1866.
(Hefting 386).

F.R. 1961-63
THE CANAL
T. H. 0.240; W. 0.325.
S.D.b.g.: Jongkind, 1877.

LINDON Alfred
(1867 - Paris, 1948)

F.R. 1961-58
STILL-LIFE (copy of an unidentified work
by Manet).
T. H. 0.22; W. 0.33.

MONET Claude

F.R. 1961-60
IN THE REGION OF HONFLEUR. SNOW
T. H. 0.815; W. 1.02.
S.b.g.: Claude Monet.
Painted in 1867.
(D.W.I. 79).

F.R. 1961-62
DRIFT-ICE ON THE SEINE AT BOUGIVAL
T. H. 0.65; W. 0.812.
S.b.d.: Claude Monet.
Painted ap. 1897?
(D.W.I. 105).

F.R. 1961-61
BREAK-UP NEAR VÉTHEUIL
(DRIFT-ICE NEAR GIVERNY)
T. H. 0.652; W. 0.93.
S.b.d.: Claude Monet.
Painted in 1880.
(D.W.I. 572).

PISSARRO Camille

F.R. 1961-67
VIEW OF PONTOISE
T. H. 0.46; W. 0.55.
S.D.b.d.: C. Pissarro 1877
(Pissarro et Venturi 388).

F.R. 1961-66
THE WATERING-PLACE, ÉRAGNY
T. H. 0.55; W. 0.65.
S.D.b.g.: C. Pissarro 95.
(Pissarro et Venturi 924).

RENOIR Pierre-Auguste

F.R. 1961-70
GIRLS READING
T. H. 0.55; W. 0.655.
S.b.d.: Renoir.
Painted ap. 1890-1895.
(Daulte 601).

F.R. 1961-72
PORTRAIT OF A WOMAN
T. H. 0.355; W. 0.272.
S.h.d.: Renoir.
Painted ap. 1890-95.
(A. Vollard, *Tableaux, pastels et dessins
de P.-A. Renoir,* 2 vols, Paris 1918, v.l. no. 508.

F.R. 1961-71
PORTRAIT OF A WOMAN SEATED
T. H. 0.35; W. 0.27.
S.h.g.: Renoir. Retouched painting.
Painted ap. 1916-1918.

SISLEY Alfred

F.R. 1961-78
THE ROAD TO MANTES
T. H. 0.38; W. 0.555.
S.D.b.d.: Sisley 74.
(Daulte 132).

F.R. 1961-76
SAINT-CLOUD
T. H. 0.508; W. 0.659.
S.D.b.d.: Sisley 77.
(Daulte 253).

F.R. 1961-77
THE WOODS AT LES ROCHES, VENEUX-NADON
T. H. 0.73; W. 0.545.
S.D.b.g.: Sisley 80.
(Daulte 408).

TOULOUSE-LAUTREC Henri de
F.R. 1961-82
G.L. DENNERY (1863-1953) painter
T. H. 0.55; W. 0.462.
S. annotated (illegible) b.g.: HTL
(intertwined monogram).
Painted ap. 1883.
(Dortu P. 223).

Non-Impressionist painters

Supplementary illustrations

AGUIAR. Houses at Auvers. 1875.

AGUIAR. Flowers in a vase. 1875.

BERNARD. Paul Gachet. 1926.

BONNARD. Blue nude. 1899-1900.

BONNARD. Home. 1920.

CALS. Self-portrait. 1851.

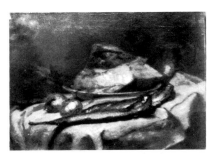

CALS. Still-life with bacon and herrings. 1870.

CALS. Sunset over Honfleur. 1873.

Supplementary illustrations

CALS. Fisherman. 1874.

CALS. Woman and child in an orchard. 1875.

CALS. Luncheon at Honfleur. 1875.

CALS. Women fraying tow. 1877.

COROT. Fishermen's houses at Sainte-Adresse. 1830.

COROT. Stranded sailing-boats at Trouville. 1830.

COROT. La Rochelle. 1851.

COROT. Tower at the water's edge. 1855-65.

COROT. The road to Sèvres. 1855-65.

COURBET. Cherry-Free blossom. 1871.

DAUBIGNY. Canal boats. 1865.

DAUMIER. The kiss. 1845.

DELACROIX. Bunch of flowers. 1849.

DERAIN. Westminster Bridge. 1906.

DERAIN. Child running on the beach.

DIAZ. Landscape. 1870.

DUBOURG. Corner of a table. 1901.

DUBOURG. Flowers. in a vase. 1910.

Supplementary illustrations

GOENEUTTE. Doctor Paul Gachet. 1891.

HELLEU. The "Nereus". 1900.

LEVY. Monsieur Guerbois. 1885.

MOREAU-NELATON. The square at Fère-en-Tardenois. (Aisne). 1886.

MURER. The Oise at l'Isle-Adam. 1903.

OSBERT. Antonin Personnaz. 1885.

OLLER Y CESTERO. By the Seine. 1875.

OLLER Y CESTERO. The student.

ROUART. The terrace by the Seine at Melun. 1880.

ROUART. San Michele Church,
near Venice. 1883.

ROUSSEAU Théodore. Morning. 1850-55.

STEVENS.
Family scene. 1880.

VAN RYSSEL Paul. The old road
at Auvers-sur-Oise. 1881.

VAN RYSSEL Paul. Apples.

VIGNON. Landscape
at Auvers-sur-Oise. 1880-85.

VIGNON. Chemin des Frileuses
at Evecquemont. 1880-85.

VLAMINCK. Still-life. 1910.

VLAMINCK. Restaurant
at Marly-le-Roi. 1905.

Supplementary illustrations

Documents (anonymous, copies, fakes)

Anonymous

19th century. Inv. 20069.
HARNESSED OXEN.
T. H. 0.46; W. 0.71.

Copies

after CÉZANNE

Paul VAN RYSSEL
pseudonym of Dr. Paul Gachet.
Lille, 1828 - Auvers-sur-Oise, 1909.

R.F. 1958-17
A MODERN OLYMPIA
T. H. 0.455; W. 0.550.
Copied from a canvas painted by Cézanne
at Auvers (R.F. 1951-31).
Presented by Paul Gachet, son of the artist, 1958.
Cat. impr. 385 b — S.A.I. 1965 — C.P.t.l. p. 386.

R.F. 1958-19
PEONIES
T. H. 0.380; W. 0.465.
Copy an unidentified painting by Cézanne.
Presented by Paul Gachet, son of the artist. 1958.
Cat. impr. 385 d — S.A.I. 1967 — C.P.t.l. p. 386.

Louis VAN RYSSEL
Pseudonym of Paul Gachet, junior.
Auvers-sur-Oise, 1873-1962.

R.F. 1958-20.
BUNCH OF DAHLIAS
T. H. 0.73; W. 0.54.
S.D.b.d.: L. Van Ryssel 06.
Inscr. b.g.: P. Cézanne.
Copy of a canvas painted by Cézanne
at Auvers (R.F. 1971).
Presented by Paul Gachet, 1958.
C.P.t.l. p. 386.

Copies

Louis VAN RYSSEL

R.F. 1958-21
BOUQUET IN A DELFT VASE
T. H. 0.41; W. 0.27.
S.D.b.g.: L. Van Ryssel 06
Inscr. b.q.: P. Cézanne.
Copy of a canvas painted at Auvers
(R.F. 1951-33).
Presented by Paul Gacher, 1958.
C.P.t.l. p. 386.

R.F. 1958-22
GREEN APPLES
T. H. 0.26; W. 0.32.
Copy of a canvas painted by Cézanne at Auvers
(R.F. 1954-6).
Presented by Paul Gachet, 1958.
C.P.t.l. p. 386.

after DEGAS

M.N.R. 848
MANZI (1849-1915).
Engraver and publisher.
T. H. 0.70; W. 0.703.
Copy.
P.A. Lemoisne reports the existence of a similar pastel, smaller in size (0.49 × 0.32, W. 995) which he dates from ap. 1890.
Attributed to the Louvre Museum by the Private Property Agency, 1951.

after PISSARRO

Paul VAN RYSSEL

R.F. 1958-18
VIEW OF LOUVECIENNES. SNOW.
T. H. 0.40; W. 0.54.
S.D.b.g.: P.V.R. 1-77.
Copy of painting by Pissarro (Pissarro and Venturi 132).
Presented by Paul Gachet, son of the artist, 1958.
Cat. impr. 385 c — S.A.I. 1966 — C.P.t.l. p. 386.

after RENOIR

M.N.R. 525
PORTRAIT OF A WOMAN
T. H. 0.415. W. 0.328.
Copy.
See the *Portrait of Alfred Sisley and his wife* painted by Renoir in 1868.
(Cologne, Wallraf-Richartz Museum).
Attributed to the Louvre Museum by the Private Property Agency, 1950.

after VAN GOGH

INV. 20621
THE LOTTERY
C. on panel. H. 0.383; W. 0.507.
Copy.
See a water-colour, touched up with gouache, by Van Gogh, 1882 (Amsterdam, Rijksmuseum V. Van Gogh).
Attributed to the Jeu de Paume Museum by the Ministry of Finance, 1973.

Supplementary illustrations

Fakes

CÉZANNE

M.N.R. 528
THE SAINTE-VICTOIRE MOUNTAIN
T. H. 0.55; W. 0.46.
S.b.d.: P. Cézanne.
Fake.
(J. Rewald, "Modern Fakes of Modern Pictures".
Art News, vol. 52 (march 1953) pp. 16-21).
Attributed to the Louvre Museum
by the Private Property Agency, 1950.

JONGKIND

M.N.R. 509
SUNSET
T. H. 0.42; W. 0.56.
S.D.b.h.: Jongkind 1858.
Extremely questionable.
Attributed to the Louvre Museum
by the Private Property Agency, 1950.

RENOIR

M.N.R. 200
SEASCAPE
T. H. 0.462; W. 0.554.
S.b.g.: Renoir.
Fake.
Attributed to the Louvre Museum
by the Private Property Agency, 1950.

M.N.R. 840
SMALL HARBOUR
T. H. 0.462; W. 0.558.
S.b.g.: Renoir.
Fake.
Attributed to the Louvre Museum
by the Private Property Agency, 1951.

SISLEY

M.N.R. 634
BRIDGE OVER THE LOING
T. H. 0.54; W. 0.65.
S.D.b.g.: Sisley 80.
Fake.
Attributed to the Louvre Museum
by the Private Property Agency, 1951.

TOULOUSE-LAUTREC

M.N.R. 524
COQUELIN AS CYRANO
T. C. H. 0.445; W. 0.30.
S.b.d. and inscription: Coquelin as Cyrano.
H.T. Lautrec (the three initials in monogram).
Fake.
(See frontispiece in colour by Aug. F. Gorguet in
Edmond Rostand: *Œuvres complètes illustrées...
Cyrano de Bergerac...* Paris, Librairie Pierre Lafitte
et cCie, s.d. [1910].
Attributed to the Louvre Museum by the Private
Property Agency, 1950.

Photos: Photographic Service
of the Union of National Museums

Dummy: Pierre Chapelot.

Photo-setting: Union Linotypiste.

Photo-engraving;
colour: Victor Michel.
black-and-white: Photogravure Point.

Printing:
Imprimerie Moderne du Lion.
First quarter 1980.